EMPOWER YOUR

— PLAN FOR THE BEST, PREPARE FOR THE WORST —

RETIREMENT

JASON & CARL CRYDERMAN

EMPOWER YOUR

— PLAN FOR THE BEST, PREPARE FOR THE WORST —

RETIREMENT

Advantage®

Published by Advantage, Charleston, South Carolina.
Member of Advantage Media Group.

ADVANTAGE is a registered trademark, and the Advantage colophon is a trademark of Advantage Media Group, Inc.

Printed in the United States of America.

10 9 8 7 6 5 4 3 2 1

ISBN: 978-1-59932-741-9
LCCN: 2021906442

Cover design by David Taylor.
Layout design by Wesley Strickland.

This publication is designed to provide accurate and authoritative information in regard to the subject matter covered. It is sold with the understanding that the publisher is not engaged in rendering legal, accounting, or other professional services. If legal advice or other expert assistance is required, the services of a competent professional person should be sought.

Advantage Media Group is proud to be a part of the Tree Neutral® program. Tree Neutral offsets the number of trees consumed in the production and printing of this book by taking proactive steps such as planting trees in direct proportion to the number of trees used to print books. To learn more about Tree Neutral, please visit **www.treeneutral.com**.

Advantage Media Group is a publisher of business, self-improvement, and professional development books and online learning. We help entrepreneurs, business leaders, and professionals share their Stories, Passion, and Knowledge to help others Learn & Grow. Do you have a manuscript or book idea that you would like us to consider for publishing? Please visit **advantagefamily.com**.

CONTENTS

ENOUGH FOR A LIFETIME

JIM AND JUDY WERE like the grandma and grandpa next door. They were in their eighties, and they always preferred that we meet with them in their home. There, on their screened back porch, they would treat us to pie and ice cream as we chatted about life and their hopes for the future. One day Judy told us she had cancer, and a few years later, she passed away.

"What will I do?" Jim asked us in his grief, but the worry lines on his face told us that practical matters were also upsetting him. "She took care of it all," he explained. "The checks, the bookkeeping, the savings and investing—she did everything like that. I didn't pay it any mind." He sighed deeply. "I don't know where to start."

We reassured him that he would be all right because we knew not only where to start but also how to ensure that his financial life would proceed smoothly. We met with him many times after that, often in his home as before, sometimes in our office. "I don't know what I would do without you guys," he told us after one of those porch sessions. "I mean ... " He paused for loss of words, but the look in

1

his eyes communicated his gratitude that we had been there for him. And then those eyes moistened with tears.

That's what it's all about for us. We are Carl and Jason Cryderman, father and son. We have been in business together in Michigan since 2001 as specialists in wealth management and retirement income planning—and we know we are in the right profession when we can offer such help.

When a spouse dies, the survivor often feels adrift. Judy had been Jim's world, but slowly he discovered he would be all right. All the financial pieces were in place so that he could move forward confidently. We reviewed all their investments with him. We helped him to combine and consolidate and simplify.

Our decade-long relationship with that couple is what made that possible. A lot of pie and ice cream went into it. Jim and Judy had shared their dreams with us, and though Jim had let her handle all the details without paying much attention to them himself, he still cared deeply about the family. Recently, his son and wife hired us to help them with their wealth management and retirement income planning as well, and they told us that one of the reasons they chose to do so was his appreciation for how we had helped his mom and dad.

In such a time of grief, people often feel burdened by the details. This should be a time to draw close to family without having to worry about finances. A relationship with the right kind of financial advisor—a fiduciary bound by law and integrity to do only what is in the client's best interest—can help to ensure that will be the case.

"Will We Have Enough?"

In our years of experience, we have repeatedly heard people express this fundamental concern: *Will we have enough money for the rest of*

our lives? How can we be sure?
Whether the prospective retiree
has millions of dollars or is living
from paycheck to paycheck,
that inner fear tends to surface
as retirement nears. We help
families overcome that fear.

In our years of experience, we have repeatedly heard people express this fundamental concern: *Will we have enough money for the rest of our lives? How can we be sure?*

Many of those who come to
see us are in their fifties, sixties,
seventies, and even eighties.
Generally, they are within five
to ten years of retirement or
already enjoying retirement. Retirement is a new phase of life. No
longer is the emphasis on accumulating money, as when they were
younger. Now they focus on protecting that money and using it for
the purposes they've set it aside for. Retirees must adjust to that reality
or their financial lives will be endangered. They need to "invest their
age," in a way that is fitting for this time of life.

Some of our clients work, or worked, in the automotive industry.
Others are from the chemical industry or are hospital employees.
Most of them are between the ages of fifty-five and seventy-five, and
their average net worth overall is between $500,000 and $2,000,000.
They are looking for an array of services, such as wealth management,
income planning, tax management, estate planning, and asset protection. The money, however, is just a part of it. The proper investment,
for example, will depend on the individual's circumstances, needs,
and goals. In our practice, and in this book, we reach out to those
who want to pull together the many elements of comprehensive,
holistic planning.

We are not offering hot tips on how to beat the market. Before investing anything, people need to make sure they have covered their short-term needs and will have an income to last a lifetime. It is great to make money in the market, but retirees should never risk more than they can afford to lose. They should set their retirement needs and their life goals and then adjust their investments to best meet them.

More Than Hope

The accumulation years are, mostly, behind the great majority of our clients. No longer do they have their noses to the grindstone. They understand the need to be working with someone who specializes in this next phase of their lives—retirement. A lot more goes into wealth management and retirement income planning than "This mutual fund averaged 8 percent over the last ten years."

The time has come for different tools for a different job. For example, a flat-head screwdriver might get the job of screwing in a Phillips-head screw done; however, it is obviously not the most efficient tool. Unfortunately, we have met a lot of families over the years that should be utilizing preservation and income-designed management philosophies and tools to most successfully get them through retirement but are still using all the accumulation tools they used to get them to retirement. They follow the accumulation philosophies, and they use accumulation advisors. Nothing is wrong with those tools, philosophies, and advisors, except that they may not be the most appropriate and efficient for preserving the wealth gained over the years and using it most wisely at this new phase of life.

We help our clients manage the many financial risks they face during what could be three decades or more of retirement. Some of their money must be kept safe and accessible, and some should be invested for a reasonable gain to offset inflation. Each objective requires the proper tools, and those will be different for every family. Some people are averse to risk; some embrace it. We try to plan for the best while making sure that we are prepared for the worst.

For each family we serve, we design a personalized Wealth Management and Retirement Income Plan. Each family has unique needs and dreams. Each has its own set of values and attitudes toward money. And each has a portfolio of assets that may or may not be realistic for the lifestyle desired. We tailor plans to make sure every family gets the right fit, not a one-size-fits-all off the rack.

Like Jim and Judy and the many others we help, you need more than hope. You want to do more than just get by. Your retirement should overflow with a lifetime of wonderful memories as you make new ones every day. What you need today is the confidence that you will be able to rekindle your dreams for that bright tomorrow—and confidence comes from taking all the proper steps in advance. By planning diligently, you can move forward with the assurance that the best is yet to be.

CHAPTER 1

WELCOME TO RETIREMENT

THE SIZE OF YOUR bank account should not be the measure of your success. Success is measured instead by the times you spend with those who are close to your heart—fulfilling dreams and building memories. It is measured by how well you have been able to accomplish what you set out to do in life. That might take the form of a grand vacation, or it might be expressed in laughter around the backyard barbecue. You could find success at the summit of Kilimanjaro, but you are just as likely to find it in a quiet conversation while fishing down at the lake.

Your money, of course, will help to determine how much you can do and how elaborate your retirement lifestyle can be, but unless you have established those plans with a determination to follow through on them, your accounts might as well be empty. They may be serving no purpose. If you lack what you love, the money will not matter. If your heart is hurting, you cannot buy joy.

Money is simply a tool to attain a vision. It is meant to support whatever lifestyle you have determined to be the ideal. Your life should control your investments, not the other way around. Money should open possibilities that make you eager to get up in the morning. It should not be keeping you awake at night.

A New Set of Concerns

Nonetheless, many people worry as they are approaching retirement. As they get well into their fifties, their priorities and approach to life feel different, and their concerns certainly are not those of a twenty-five-year-old. Most people have been accustomed to working and saving since their teenage days, back when the years seemed to stretch endlessly ahead. Time seemed to be in bountiful supply. In the resilience of youth, they could invest more aggressively and take more risks.

And then comes the prospect of retirement. No longer will your focus be so much on contributing to your investments. You'll be less likely to swing for the fences for maximum gain. You will be thinking more about how much you could lose. The time has come to live on what you have been setting aside. You must replace that paycheck with a retirement income, and you might need that cash flow to continue for as many years as you spent on the job, or more.

> **How have you prepared for the unemployment of retirement? This reality often leads to a shift in mindset—and it should also lead to a shift in investment style.**

The fact that you will no longer be working for your pay changes your perspective. You now will depend on your savings and investments to do the work for you. You therefore are likely feeling protective of your nest egg and less inclined to take the big risks. You do not want to retire just to see the market claim a third of your savings and force you to get a job again. Think of it this way: if that were to happen, you would have given up a third of the retirement lifestyle you anticipated, a third of the things you loved and cared about, because of the value that was lost. A good indicator of success in retirement is for you to control your investments, income, and lifestyle—not Wall Street.

In essence, you are facing a long stretch—typically, twenty, thirty years or more—of unemployment. It may be voluntary unemployment, but it is unemployment nonetheless. You will get a small jobless benefit in the form of Social Security, and may have some form of company pension—but what will go along with that? When you no longer can rely on those forty hours' worth of wages each week, where will the income come from to live the awesome retirement you've always dreamed about and deserve? How have you prepared for the unemployment of retirement? This reality often leads to a shift in mindset—and it should also lead to a shift in investment style. As fiduciary advisors that focus on wealth management and retirement income planning for retirees, we help people to get through those years successfully and to ease the stress and worries that people so often face at this stage of life—moving into and through an awesome retirement.

It can be quite a challenge. How do you produce the best possible retirement income on what you have put away? If you have half a million dollars, that is not what you will be living on. It simply will not last. Instead, that is what you have available to produce the income that you will be living on. You will want a regular and reliable cash flow to replace the paycheck for as long as you live. In effect, you need to use your savings to recreate the pension that most people retiring these days will not be getting from their employer. In Chapter 8 we will examine strategies to produce a guaranteed lifelong income from your years of savings and investments.

If you are nearing retirement age, your concerns in life most certainly have changed significantly from those you had when you were starting out. In those days it might have seemed as if you could wait until tomorrow to put that money away. As the years went by, however, time got shorter for both you and your money. But if you followed a regular discipline of saving and investing, that money likely grew significantly.

Time was your biggest asset when you were younger, and you could afford more aggressive investments and more risk. It takes years for money to work its magic through growth and compounding, but when left to grow, it can double and double again. You can make a lot of money even through relatively modest but continuous investments. Nearing retirement, however, you no longer have those accumulation years ahead of you. Like a lot of families we serve, you may find yourself needing to tap into your savings and investments for income.

If all of your money is still in the market, you can be at the mercy of its unpredictable and often severe fluctuations. You might have less opportunity to recover from a market crash—and if the tough years in the economy come early in your retirement, while you need to make withdrawals, your lifestyle can suffer. Then, when the economy recovers, you may still be likely to invest more conservatively, further limiting your gains.

You also must pay more attention now to inflation than you did when you were younger. In your working and accumulating years, you likely got regular promotions and raises that kept up with inflation. But as you look back, you can see how things progressively became more expensive. What did you pay for a loaf of bread or a gallon of gas twenty or thirty years ago? What will you be paying twenty or thirty years from now? As retirees live increasingly longer, the toll of inflation must not be underestimated. In retirement you may have to create your own raises to deal with the ever-increasing cost of living. Therefore, even as you are looking to invest more conservatively, you cannot invest *too* conservatively. At an absolute minimum, your portfolio needs to keep ahead of inflation.

It is also likely that you will be thinking more about taxes than you once did. Young people send in their tax forms in April, and they either pay some money in or get a refund, and that's about it. If they are in a high tax bracket, they may even see that as a good sign that they are making more money. Retirees, however, feel a lot of pressure for more tax efficiency with their investments. They tend to look to secure a lifelong income while sending as little as possible to the government. They want to be in the lowest possible tax bracket, drawing efficiently from income sources to maintain that lower tax rate status. It's like golf: the lowest score wins.

In Chapters 5 and 6, we will take a closer look at the financial risks and tax scenarios that you should consider to ensure a successful and happy retirement.

Troubles in the Transition

Not all the stresses of planning for a successful and happy retirement are financial in nature. Many people are not prepared for how they will feel when they no longer are getting up and going off to a job every day. They might have imagined that in their retirement they would inaugurate a life of leisure, relaxing in the hammock or playing with the grandkids when they are not playing golf or chatting with old friends on the veranda.

The realities can be somewhat different. Sometimes spouses can get on each other's last nerve when they suddenly find themselves both around the house all day. If the relationship is sound, those extra hours can be joyful. But more time together also means more time for disagreements. Any time of transition can accentuate tensions. If the couple already has issues, those added hours might not add up to more togetherness.

For retirees who lack an active social life or hobbies and other outside interests, boredom can set in. When their hind ends get sore from holding down the couch, they may find themselves actually missing the workplace and the nine-to-five routine. At least then they were occupied, without hours of free time to contemplate how they should be spending it. At least then they felt they had a purpose in life and were contributing. They felt connected and part of something bigger. They felt valued as part of a team.

And those who do find plenty of things to occupy their time may be surprised that they need every bit as much money as they did before retiring. It is not what they expected. We have found that particularly in the first five to ten years of retirement, many people fill their newfound free time with activities that can be expensive. They no longer are in the workplace earning money. Instead, they are taking trips and spending money. If the couple goes away for the weekend, they might stay longer than when they were still working, since there's no need to return to work Monday morning.

This can also be the stage of life when people begin to experience an increasing number of health issues. They worry about the cost of healthcare and the potential that they might need long-term care at some point. We will examine those issues in more detail in Chapter 7.

As people age through life, they also begin to have thoughts about their legacy. What will they be leaving for their children and grandchildren? Those tend not to be the sort of concerns that preoccupy younger people. In leaving a legacy, older people are often thinking about more than the money. They want to feel that they have led a life of significance and purpose, and they begin to consider how their life savings might contribute to a better world for their heirs or even charities, and not just to a bigger portfolio for them. We will look at estate and legacy planning in Chapter 9.

The Right Tools for the Task

Meeting the challenges of retirement very well may require a different set of tools than you used when you were younger and maybe working with a stockbroker. Accumulation tools and philosophies may have been in your best interest for your working and accumulation years. The advisors who specialized in growth and accumulation may have been right for you then. They may have helped to get you to this point, when you have accumulated your wealth and are ready to retire.

Over the years we have often seen an unfortunate disconnect, however, among a lot of prospective clients who come in to see us. We ask them about their retirement goals and dreams. We ask about their desired lifestyle. How do they think and feel about money? How would it affect them if another 2008 came along, or the beginning of 2020, and they were to lose 30 percent or more of their portfolio? Would that disrupt their successful and happy retirement lifestyle? Most tell us that such a thing must never happen to them again—not in their retirement. They tell us that they have learned to think differently about their hard-earned money. But when we look at their portfolio, we often identify that disconnect between their retirement goals and their money—they are employing the same growth and accumulation tools and philosophy they were using in the past. It has been said that the definition of insanity is doing the same thing repeatedly while expecting different results. Many people engage in that sort of insanity when it comes to investing, and it can severely impact a successful retirement.

As you contemplate retirement, you should consider transitioning out of accumulation mode and into more appropriate management and tools for the years of retirement ahead. Accumulation management and tools may have brought you to this point; however, they may not be the most appropriate for your successful retirement, simply because they may bring unnecessary levels of risk exposure and losses to your hard-earned money. In working with our most successful families, we have found that using the *right* tools for the job is essential. You need the right philosophies, advisors, and investment products to help you achieve the successful and happy retirement you deserve.

You don't have to settle for an all-purpose broker. A bricklayer can install a strong foundation for your house, but is that the right skill for building a roof? If you are like many people, the financial advisor with whom you have worked for years may no longer be appropriate for your retirement phase of life. Quite often he or she has helped you for decades, focusing on growth and accumulation, and may even have become a good friend. The time may have come, however, to think in a more preservation- and income-minded way about your money and move away from that mindset of maximum growth and such high exposure to risk. But how do you say goodbye to that nice guy or gal who has been a big part of your financial life? You may be thinking you now need to preserve your money and develop an income stream from it, not just accumulate more and more, and you may find your current advisor is unlikely or unable to switch gears with you—away from growth and accumulation and more into preservation and income. Over the years we've found that as good at growth and accumulation as some advisors may be, helping families most appropriately manage their money for preservation and income just may not be their specialty.

Your life has evolved into a whole new phase—your awesome retirement—and so should your financial management and strategies. You might have built a great relationship with your broker, but at some point it may be in your best interest to shake hands respectfully and move on. We understand your position and concerns. We have heard them expressed by people just like you, from our most successful families, many times. In this book we will share with you some strategies and solutions to ensure you will have a good understanding of what you should do to have a financially successful and happy retirement.

CHAPTER 2

WHERE ARE YOU HEADING?

THINK OF YOUR RETIREMENT as a road trip, a new adventure. One day you will be getting into your retirement car, closing the doors, turning the ignition key, and cruising off into, hopefully, a long and successful retirement.

The best way to get to your destination is to look straight ahead through the windshield in the direction you're heading. The families we serve succeed by following our advice to focus on where they are going and the view ahead instead of what they've done in the past, where they've been, and what is in the rearview mirror. If you spend a lot of time focusing on the past, not only could you miss the awesome opportunities and scenery ahead—the dreams you are striving to fulfill—but you may also find it difficult to maneuver life's potholes and detours.

Retirement planning is about both the journey and the destination. You need to get a clear look at the lifestyle you want. That starts with becoming fully aware of exactly where you are now and the best route to your destination. Instead of looking back at where you were a decade ago, or even just a couple of years ago, and how you got to this point, ask yourself how you can pursue your goals while managing your money most appropriately and efficiently for this next phase of your life. We should always learn from our past—what has worked and what has not—but be careful not to get stuck in it.

These are the kinds of questions you should be asking: Why do you own what you own? What is its purpose? Where will it take you? What experiences do you want to have? Are you doing everything you can to take control of your financial future for a successful retirement?

One of the first things we ask all the families we serve is: What do you love? Tell us what you truly care about—what you are excited about when you get up in the morning? What are your dreams and passions for your retirement? If you could close your eyes and envision the Norman Rockwell painting of your perfect retirement, who and what would be in it? What would you be doing? What does your picture-perfect retirement journey look like?

Consider how you would paint that scene, because your retirement plan should be built around that image. Based on what you want to achieve, you should use only the tools, philosophies, and advisors that will enhance your opportunities to realize those goals. Your dreams should dictate how you invest. They should not be at the mercy of how you invest.

To the Heart of the Matter

What is life all about in retirement? This is a question that people are increasingly asking themselves as they approach and head into retirement. This is also a very common discussion we have with people during our initial visits. The answer will have everything to do with the decisions they make as we help them design their version of a Financial Empowerment Plan.

Financial planning encompasses so much more than investments, although that certainly is a major part of it. However, a comprehensive approach includes broader topics of estate planning, tax planning, income planning, and risk management, and we will examine all those elements in the chapters ahead.

Your dreams should dictate how you invest. They should not be at the mercy of how you invest.

Above all, your Financial Empowerment Plan should be designed just for you. Your neighbor's financial plan is not yours, nor is your coworker's or your golfing buddy's, no matter how enthusiastically they proclaim how well they are doing. Their families, their goals, their dreams and visions for retirement are very likely not the same as yours. Your Financial Empowerment Plan should be custom-built to help you achieve your unique goals and dreams for your awesome and successful retirement.

If you and your spouse were to decide today that you were going to take a trip from coast to coast, you would probably use a GPS, or Google Maps, and start planning some of the places you would like to see and experience along your journey. You would try to develop a sensible schedule for where and when you would be in which towns and at which hotels. You would organize your journey to get the most out of it.

Likewise, when you jump into your retirement car and look out the front window, you need a financial road map or GPS to help guide you along your journey. Instead of wondering what's next, you should have an idea of what's out there and have a plan for how to maneuver along the way—for bad weather, traffic jams, and even detours.

We have helped many families navigate their happy and successful retirement route. Mile marker by mile marker, we help them enjoy the trip as they work their way to their destinations, and when they do face those detours, we help them navigate the best way around them. Some have told us we are like their guides for their retirement trip.

How would you envision a successful retirement? We spend a lot of time on that question in our initial visits with the families we serve. If they say they want to do a lot of traveling, what does that look like? If they say they would like to spend time with family, what is involved in that? We need to know what their retirement truly looks like so we can help build their very own personalized Financial Empowerment Plan.

We have never had anyone tell us, "Well, my dream is to make more and more money and just keep building my portfolio bigger and bigger." In our experience, people are generally in pursuit of something with more depth and fulfillment than just making more money. Most of the families we have worked with are at a point where they want to finally reap the benefits of all their hard years of working and start truly enjoying a happy and successful retirement. Younger people tend to be more impulsive, but we've found that retirement-age people tend to think more with their hearts. Their thoughts often turn to legacy and philanthropy, to family and worthy pursuits and the things that they love and will fulfill their lives in retirement. They are in search of purpose. They want to leave their mark.

The Risk of Not Knowing

Over the years we've met people who just don't seem to know where to start shaping their road map for a successful retirement. Some retirees just stumble through retirement not really knowing what they can afford to do. They tend to lack a grasp on their finances, so they really don't know whether they have a reasonable chance of reaching their destination of accomplishing their retirement dreams. Some investors have dreams that are way out of line with the amount of money they have saved in their portfolio. They tend to overindulge themselves during retirement and often get into financial trouble along the way. Other investors might be in great financial shape but are so accustomed to a life of saving, not spending, and fearful of losing it all that they might miss out on awesome retirement memories. All of these scenarios are the unfortunate side effects of not knowing and not planning appropriately for a happy and successful retirement.

We often relate what we call "The Tale of Two Brothers—Bob and Joe" to illustrate the need for effective planning. Both Bob and Joe retired on the same day in 2005, and both had $500,000 in each of their portfolios, and both took the exact amount of income out of their accounts during retirement. Bob worked closely with his spouse in aligning their dreams and visions of their retirement, transitioning to an efficient preservation and income-driven mindset and philosophy and using appropriate tools, advisors, and management methods. Joe, on the other hand, relied on his longtime broker, who also happened to be his golf buddy—"He's always done me right, and we'll get through this together." Three years later, after both had experienced the devastation of 2008, Bob's portfolio had risen to $800,000, while Joe's portfolio was down to $200,000. As you can imagine, he was not exactly looking at the retirement of his dreams, but rather the unfortunate results of failing to build an efficient Financial Empowerment Plan.

Organizing Your Priorities

As you approach retirement, it is time to organize your priorities and design your ideal retirement picture of attaining your retirement goals. Since they're an important part of your financial planning, it is good idea to write them down. Who and what is important to you? Is there anyone or any cause that you would wish to support? What are your travel plans? Would you like to pursue further education or even a second career? How about hobbies? What makes you feel fulfilled and happy? What are your goals as a couple to continue developing that lifelong relationship?

These are just a few of the fundamental questions that will help you organize your retirement priorities, and asking them is a vital step for a happy and successful retirement.

In our experience, most retirees spend more money in the first several years of retirement, and then their spending tends to slow down. We have observed that more times than not, people spend just as much, if not more, during the first ten years or so in retirement than they did before retiring. The hours that they used to spend at work are now leisure hours that they fill with activities. Traveling, whether to Paris or to see the grandkids just a few hours away, costs money. A round of golf and a round of drinks are not free. People often head into retirement with a bucket list of long-postponed desires that they want to fulfill while they are young enough and healthy enough. Hopefully, with proper planning, they are wealthy enough, and remain so.

As you identify your retirement goals, it's also important to make sure they are realistic and attainable. It's not uncommon when we ask people to share their budget with us that they don't actually have a written budget but rather figure they must be okay because they have some money left at the end of the month. Not having a written budget and payment plan, and not knowing how much money goes where and what will be left for their retirement goals, can prevent those goals from being realistic and attainable.

As fiduciary advisors focusing on wealth management and income in retirement, we work closely with the families we represent on building and tracking budgets and income sources. How much money do you need for essential expenses, what we often call "must-haves," and how much do you need for nonessential expenses, known as "want-to-haves." In retirement, those wants can increase tremendously as you look to fulfill your dreams and build memories. "I don't know how I ever had time to work!" retirees often tell us. "I'm so busy now doing all the things that I love and care about and always dreamed of doing in retirement, and we definitely wouldn't be living such a happy and successful retirement without having a written budget and income plan."

Therefore, your household budget in retirement should provide more discretionary spending money for those extras that you will now have extra time to enjoy—and that amount is likely to be more than you anticipated. Designing a plan to fit those additional expenses into your budget will help you determine whether your goals and dreams are realistic and attainable. Having a written plan will help you avoid being that brother who just figured it would all be okay.

People often tell us they intend to travel more in retirement, and that, of course, means they may tend to spend more money too. As their advisors, it is our responsibility to account for this extra spending in their retirement planning to help them feel comfortable knowing their retirement dreams will be attainable without causing financial misfortune. In retirement the withdrawal rate from your portfolio also needs to be reasonable and realistic. You need to be certain that you will not just reach your destination but, more importantly, that you fulfill your retirement dreams and enjoy the journey of a happy and successful retirement along the way. You only get one shot at retirement, and you can't afford to get it wrong—it's our goal to help you get it right!

As you organize your priorities, start with your goals and dreams, and then build a financial plan and budget designed to accomplish them. It's important to have a formal written plan, utilizing and leveraging all of your available resources and tools, that will help you make the most of your happy and successful retirement.

Organizing Your Paperwork

It's important that your goals, as well as your written Financial Empowerment Plan, are in good order. As we build a relationship with the families we serve, we examine their current plans, if they have them, and all of their financial records to help them organize their financial life. This includes tax returns, employer-sponsored retirement and/or pension plans, and all other investment accounts, like 401(k)s, IRAs, Roths, brokerage accounts, and bank or credit union accounts. Quite often we will also review other information, like estate-planning documentation—the trusts, wills, and other papers—as well as their health, life, and long-term-care insurance coverage, as these all play vital roles in an overall written plan.

It's not uncommon for families to not be able to locate all of their documents when we first meet, especially those that haven't been very organized yet. Some tell us that they don't even open their investment statements when they come in the mail; they just file them away. Organizing and simplifying their financial life are just two of the benefits the families we work with have told us they truly appreciate. Once we start working with families, they will become more organized, and we help them get a much clearer view of their overall finances. This is extremely valuable not only for them but also, one day, for their successors and heirs when they will have to settle their estate. If your finances are in a state of disarray, you could be leaving your loved ones with headaches, hassles, and unjustified time and expenses in settling your estate.

Through our holistic planning approach, we are able to offer families the reassurance that their finances will not only be organized and simplified for them while they are alive but also flow smoothly if and when something happens to them. We make sure that the surviving spouse and/or the children know and understand the goals and wishes of your Financial Empowerment Plan and that your wealth is transferred with maximum efficiency.

Time to Take Action

We understand that custom-tailoring your family's version of a Financial Empowerment Plan can seem overwhelming at times. Comprehensive and long-term financial planning can often involve difficult family issues and sensitive topics of discussion. And frankly, holistic planning at some point means addressing one's potential failing health and mortality, neither of which make for easy conversation, which can unfortunately lead people to procrastinate, ultimately making matters worse.

We worked with a gentleman who was preparing to retire after thirty years with the same company, and we wanted to ensure his beneficiary designations were in order. He assured us that the beneficiary of his retirement account was his wife, as he hadn't changed that since he had been hired almost three decades ago. Just to be sure, we made a quick call by speakerphone to the human resources department and asked who was named as his primary beneficiary. We heard the answer loud and clear: "Nobody." Our client just about flew out of his seat. As you can imagine, this was a huge surprise to him and his wife, and she asked in a panic, "I'm not your beneficiary, dear?" We don't doubt that he had named her as his primary beneficiary in the original paperwork, but we learned that the company had changed its computer software several times over the years and this was an unfortunate result of such changes. We immediately helped get his beneficiaries updated, which he said had sealed their trust in us for life.

You cannot take anything for granted. We highly suggest double-checking these types of things as a matter of due diligence and help all of the families we work with to do so. If he had died without his beneficiary updated, over $400,000 in his 401(k) plan would have had to be settled in probate court. Eventually, the money would most likely have made it to his wife, since nobody else was listed, but it still would have been an expensive, unfortunate, and unacceptable headache for her. We've heard of other situations where a hostile ex-spouse was still listed as the beneficiary of accounts—as you can imagine, such an oversight can be devastating. It is so easy to get it right before it comes to that simply by doing a complete and thorough beneficiary review, which is a standard part of our holistic planning process.

Often the consequences of procrastination are more of an annoyance than a nightmare.

We worked with a widow who was having trouble getting the title for a pickup truck that her husband had purchased several years before he died. He had paid it off, but he had not taken the time to find out why the state had not sent the title—and the credit union had since been sold. The widow needed to hire an attorney to find the records and get the title in her name. It was a mess, and it was one of those matters that can too easily be forgotten about and slip through the cracks, causing unneeded hassles and headaches later.

Most people tell us that dealing with such issues is not their vision of their ideal retirement and is just one of the many reasons why they want to work with us. Nor do they dream of sitting down for several hours a day watching the markets, examining their portfolio, and trying to analyze trends to figure out what and when they should buy or sell. Some people might thrive on that, but they are not the type who tend to seek our services. We work with people who want to enjoy life doing other things in retirement. They want to know that when they lay their head on the pillow, they have a solid, written plan in place that is driven by their goals, that is designed to protect and grow their investments, and that will leave their time free to fulfilling their retirement dreams.

CHAPTER 3

FILLING THE INCOME GAP

"How many people here still have a pension?" we sometimes ask when we speak at community events. Fewer and fewer people raise their hands. Not long ago it might have been three times as many, but pensions clearly are going by the wayside.

Pensions once were the foundation of retirement income and security. An employee might work for a company forty years and have a guaranteed income for life. Unfortunately, that is all changing. Not too many years ago, General Motors and Ford had the largest pension buyback in US history, and we've since seen the same from other companies across the US as well.

We look at income in retirement like a three-legged stool designed to support your lifestyle. One leg may be your pension, the second generally is Social Security, and the third leg is your own investments and savings. Your retirement income stool should be comfortable and sturdy. Today, however, the pension leg may be missing for many, and the Social Security leg feels uncertain at best—which leaves that one leg of your personal savings and investments to hold up and support your retirement lifestyle. More and more people are likely to end up tipping over, with their retirement lifestyle falling to the floor unless they make the appropriate changes in how they think about and invest in retirement.

Goodbye to Pensions

A lot of companies have offered buyouts to avoid the commitment of paying pensions, possibly for decades. The buyout could be a lump sum of several hundred thousand dollars that the retiree can invest to create his or her own personal pension. If handled wisely, that lump sum can become quite a blessing to the surviving spouse and a financial legacy for the children.

Though pensions are disappearing, other options have been evolving to fill the gap in guaranteed lifetime income that most retirees want and deserve. We help families create their own personalized pensions using some of the assets they've invested over the years. When this is done right, they can get a regular paycheck for as long as they live, and anything left over will pass to the spouse and possibly to the next generations as well. We can show them some unique concepts, strategies, and tools that will make that possible. In Chapter 8 we will take a closer look at income planning for retirement.

Only a generation or so ago, people didn't necessarily think this way. The responsibility was on their employer to contribute to a defined-benefit plan, their pension, to provide a majority of the income they would need to support their retirement lifestyle. Whatever else they could save was just extra. They didn't have to give as much thought to doing their own investing and income planning, and they would still have reasonable guaranteed cash flow during retirement.

Today is the age of the 401(k) retirement plans. They came about in the late 1970s via a provision added to the IRS code for tax-deferred savings. Companies saw this as a means to escape their pension obligations, as many realized they had massive but under-funded liabilities. How could they pay all those people for all those years, especially after they were no longer working and an asset to the company? Employers were looking for a way out of this long-term responsibility and obligation, and the defined contribution plans—401(k)—was that opportunity.

As a result, corporate America has been moving en masse to dump the traditional pensions, known as defined-benefit plans, and adopt the 401(k)s, or defined contribution plans. Retirees who are expecting a lifelong stream of payments may be offered buyouts, and they sometimes see their benefits slashed. The responsibility for retirement savings and guaranteed lifetime income has shifted away from the employer and directly to the employee. If you are lucky, the company might match a small portion of your contributions to the investment account.

Without traditional pensions many retirees have to fend for themselves on Social Security and whatever they have set aside in their own savings and investments. All too often what they saved could be little to nothing. We have seen this happening more and more as some workers live paycheck to paycheck, living for today without saving and investing for tomorrow—their retirement years.

Nonetheless, 401(k)s and similar retirement savings plans do offer some nice benefits. Employees can defer taxes on the portion of their income that they contribute. They get an immediate tax break, and the money can grow in their account for decades without incurring additional taxes until withdrawn during retirement. In other words, instead of paying, say, a 20 percent tax up front on a dollar of income and netting 80 cents of the dollar, employees can invest the full dollar without paying the tax up front, magnifying the power of compounding growth on 100 percent of the money. Meanwhile, if they get a matching contribution from their employer, that's like free money added to their account.

The evolution of retirement planning over the past generation from the pension era to the 401(k) era has helped many people save for a fruitful retirement. The benefits of employer matching and tax deferral can be a powerful part of a retiree's overall wealth management and retirement income plan. In addition, employees can potentially borrow against their 401(k) account and, under limited circumstances, tap into their account earlier than other types of IRAs and avoid the 10 percent early withdrawal penalty. Neither of those benefits is available with a traditional pension.

What about Social Security?

Clearly, the Social Security leg of the retirement income stool is losing its strength. When the Social Security Act of 1935 was instituted, few people lived more than a few years beyond the set age to receive Social Security, which was sixty-five, and many died without collecting any income from Social Security at all. For many years the number of workers contributing into Social Security far outweighed the number of retirees and the amount of money that was being withdrawn. More recently, however, with life expectancy much greater, the population of older folks drawing Social Security income much larger, and fewer young workers contributing to the system, the future of Social Security is no doubt in question.

The system was not designed to do what it must accomplish today, so we have seen politicians trying to make changes to it. We have seen, for example, the gradual increase on taxation of benefits, which originally were not supposed to be taxed at all. Today, up to 85 percent of our Social Security benefit can be subject to income tax. You paid a hefty tax for years so that someday you could receive that benefit, and now you might pay a hefty tax when you finally receive it.

The government is in a position similar to the one that corporations faced as they wondered how they ever could afford to continue making those guaranteed lifetime pension payments. With the baby boomer generation retiring in droves and living longer, while fewer people pay into the system, something has to give, which has in the past and could again lead to the government playing with the numbers, trying to keep Social Security income benefits from running out. Recently we've seen Congress chip away at the potential benefits by eliminating some popular filing methods that would allow husbands and wives to maximize their lifetime income by strategically filing. There's a pretty good chance more changes are coming. We could possibly see Social Security taxes increase, the amount of monthly benefits go down, the retirement age to receive benefits go up, or even the implementation of means testing—which means the amount of your income benefit would depend on how much the government decides you need. The ultimate solution, from the government's perspective, is to do what a lot of corporations have done with pensions and shift the burden and

> **With life expectancy much greater, the population of older folks drawing Social Security income much larger, and fewer young workers contributing to the system, the future of Social Security is no doubt in question.**

responsibility of a guaranteed monthly paycheck for life onto the individual.

Many people ask whether Social Security will continue to be there for them when they retire. We believe Social Security income benefits will most likely always be there as a source of income in retirement. However, as we've indicated earlier, there are likely to be changes coming to Social Security taxes and income. Our thoughts are that those who already are collecting benefits when any changes do occur will be likely to see fewer changes than those who haven't begun collecting yet. Some possible changes we could see for those already receiving benefits could be fewer cost-of-living adjustments and more taxation of benefits, and just those two aspects can seriously erode the value of the Social Security income benefit.

Prospective retirees often wonder whether they should claim their benefit as early as possible, at age sixty-two, or wait until their full retirement age or longer to get a bigger monthly payment. The longer you wait, the more your income benefit increases—between about 5 to 8 percent, depending on your age, up until you reach age seventy. Unfortunately, there is no easy, one-size-fits-all answer. This is an individual family decision that depends upon many factors. Do you need the money for living expenses? What other sources of guaranteed lifetime income will you have? How much of your Social Security income will be taxable? How is your health, and how long do people tend to live in your family?

Another big question we ask the families we represent is whether they intend to continue working in any capacity after triggering their Social Security income benefit. This is extremely important, because until full retirement age, earning too much income can significantly reduce the benefit. For 2020, the income limit was $18,240, or $1,520 a month. For every two dollars that you earn above that, you lose a dollar of your Social Security benefit. If you are at full retirement age or older, the amount you can earn is unlimited.

When you choose to trigger your Social Security retirement income benefit is not a decision you should make after spending a few minutes on the Social Security website and doing a few calculations, nor should you just do what your brother or sister or friend did. You should run the numbers with a retirement income specialist who can advise you whether it would make the most sense to collect your Social Security benefit at sixty-two, sixty-six, seventy, or anytime in between. The goal is to maximize the Social Security income for both you and your spouse while maintaining a cash flow that you can comfortably live on. You could get a bigger chunk of change by waiting, but many people want the money while they are younger and more likely to enjoy it.

If you do wait to take your benefit, what happens if you don't live long enough to collect your Social Security at all, or at least live long enough to collect enough to break even? Another unfortunate fact about Social Security is that when one spouse passes away, the surviving spouse only gets to keep the bigger of the two benefits, with the government keeping the balance of the smaller benefit that has yet to be paid out. When both spouses pass away, the government is the only beneficiary—they keep 100 percent of any and all payments and funds that you may have paid into Social Security but weren't fortunate enough to live long enough to get.

Again, for the most successful families we serve, it's not just about the money. It's about their image of what retirement will be like. How much income will they need to meet their goals, and what will be the sources of that income? In the case of some families, when they answer that question, it will be clear that they should claim their benefit at age sixty-two. There may be less income from Social Security, but they feel they will get more bang for those bucks. Others will find a huge advantage in waiting until seventy. In our experience, no two families are alike.

It is a big decision, and it must not be made lightly just because you get a letter from the Social Security office saying you can now flip on that switch. The employees who work for the Social Security Administration, although we are sure they are very nice people, are not professionally licensed to provide good financial advice. You may not want to depend on them to help you figure out what is in your family's best interest in your overall retirement income plan. Truthfully, that is really not their job.

You have contributed a small fortune over the years into Social Security, so it's important to consider everything that could influence your decision on when to begin collecting your benefit. That decision could have a lot to do with the retirement lifestyle you desire, your health status, longevity, and other income sources. You may need more information than you will get from spending a few minutes with a clerk or browsing a website. Social Security employees can probably answer some general questions, but they are not a planning service. In our opinion it would be more in your best interest to work with someone who knows you, your circumstances, and your retirement dreams and goals.

Staying the Course

As you can see, the third leg of the traditional retirement stool—your own savings and investments—could play a much larger role in your annual and overall lifetime income plan. The way you manage that responsibility can make or break your retirement. A lot of people have acknowledged and expressed to us that they do not really have the time, inclination, or experience and knowledge in investing into and through retirement to do this themselves. They understand the importance, but managing financial affairs is not particularly what they want to be thinking about and spending all of their time on during retirement.

That is another reason to develop a good relationship with someone you can trust, someone who cares about you and isn't just out to sell you something, and someone who by law must put your best interest first. Time is of the essence. Even if you feel that you are getting a late start, there still could be a lot you can do if you work with the right tools and with the right advisor toward your clearly defined goals. The objectives and outcomes for investing and income planning in retirement tend to be different than when you were accumulating your wealth. It is up to you to adapt and seek the right advisors, advice, and tools so that you can stay on course to the successful retirement of your dreams.

CHAPTER 4

A TEAM YOU CAN TRUST

WHEN WORKING WITH FAMILIES on their version of a personalized Financial Empowerment Plan, it often seems as if we are solving a jigsaw puzzle together. Generally, the completer and more holistic the plan, the more pieces and the more complicated the pieces may be to fit together, and just like any properly completed puzzle, the pieces can't just be forced into place. All aspects of a complete and holistic plan need to be lined up, planned out, and compared to the big picture—your vision and dreams of a happy, successful retirement. Each piece plays a vital role in the success of your overall plan, whether it be your budget, investments, insurances, wills, trusts, taxes, or income sources, and your personalized Financial Empowerment Plan will help ensure the happiness and success of your awesome retirement.

It's really as if we are helping align the pieces to the puzzles that people have been bringing to us for decades. They have built and accumulated many different pieces of their overall plan over the years, so that at some point they would be able to sit down and figure out how to make the connections of putting their formal wealth management and retirement income plan together. In their minds they have some idyllic image for their future—the vision of their happiest and most successful retirement, truly a picture on the puzzle box that is different for each of us.

As fiduciary advisors we work hand in hand with families to help align those pieces so that they can see it all coming together. We don't want them to get close to their big picture of retirement just to find that a piece or two is missing or needs to be forced and jammed into place. We want to help them build their Financial Empowerment Plan with confidence and excitement.

> **In retirement, you need your coaches and teammates to be working together on the same formal game plan to get you into and through a successful season.**

Some families have told us we are like the head coach of a football team. Quite often the team also has an offensive coach, a running back coach, a wide receiver coach, and others. Someone needs to pull them all together. When the coach calls a play, the team members cannot be running in random directions, or the whole game will be one big fumble. The same is true with your team of advisors. They all need to be on the same playbook page—you can't afford a financial fumble at this phase of your life.

In retirement, you need your coaches and teammates to be working together on the same formal game plan to get you into and through a successful season. As you approach retirement, everything might feel as if it is in place and you have reached your goals—and then you realize that basically you are facing a long stretch of unemployment. This is not the time to wish you had done better. This is the time to be comfortable and confident that everything in your plan is working in concert. The right coaches and the right game plan will get you to your goal line of your awesome retirement.

Advice You Can Do Without

Unfortunately, we've seen some investors frequently get their advice in the wrong places. Many have been doing it on their own or don't really have a team they can trust. In fact, when it comes to retirement investments and income, honestly some just don't know where to start.

Sometimes investors' notions of retirement planning amount to watching what their coworkers do or following what friends and neighbors recommend. They get their financial advice from sources who lack expertise or whose personal situations and motivations may be worlds apart from their own. Consequently, they might not take the appropriate actions to ensure that they will have sufficient money set aside to get them through a long, awesome retirement.

Your work colleagues might be intelligent in their own way, but what is right for them may not necessarily be what is right for you. If you are sixty years old, the perspective of a thirty-year-old who is starting a family and saving for a house is unlikely to reflect where you are in life. Even someone about the same age as you will likely have an entirely different financial situation. He or she may be considering early retirement for very good reasons, whereas it might not make as much sense for you.

Nor will you be getting personalized advice from the media. Those talking heads and commentators do not know you or what is in your family's best interest. They do know that advertisers are paying to talk to a particular demographic. They dispense information for the masses, and it is not gospel for everybody. In fact, the media tends to play up the emotions of fear and greed because that is what attracts attention and increases ratings. It is in their best interest to make you feel unsettled so that you want to read to the next page, listen further, or even call the number they're giving out. Advertising and investing both have a way of playing on emotions. Investors need to set emotions aside to avoid big mistakes.

Some investors in recent years have turned to online "robo-advisors," thinking they can get cheap advice that will still be worthwhile. How many robots do you know that are personable and can talk to you about your family's goals and dreams? We like to think that the personal touch still matters. When they are surfing the internet, some people seem unable to distinguish what might be valuable. They are buried by information overload. Choose any financial term and perform an online search, and you will be offered hundreds to thousands of pages that you potentially could read and get lost in. How is anyone to digest all that? This often leads to analysis paralysis, where it's too much information, not enough concrete advice that's truly in your best interest, and the outcome generally leads to doing nothing at all.

Temptations are everywhere to chase the next hot thing. That is a good way to stray off track in your retirement planning. People have lost fortunes chasing after what we call the "perfect silver bullet investment"—which in our experience simply does not exist. Instead, the rational approach is to research whether a prospective theory or investment lines up with your goals and best interest. In our experience, the more you can have personal relations, building rapport and trust with real life advisors, the more comfortable and confident you will be with our personalized Financial Empowerment Plan.

We're sure you have heard the late-night pitches on TV: "Buy gold now! Don't wait, or you'll be sorry!" Unless you go to your personal financial advisor before you act and talk these decisions through in light of your own situation, you will likely end up with a lot of regrets. You can be sure that whoever is making those TV pitches doesn't necessarily have your best interest at heart as much as they are simply pushing and selling as much of their product as they possibly can.

Delegating to Your Team

Some investors have had the experience of running a business or have been in a managerial position where they are in charge of others. They know how to delegate. They usually know that they do not know it all and can't possibly be most efficient and successful trying to do it all without help from others. Good leaders surround themselves with experts in various fields. If you are in charge of your family's finances, you should also delegate various areas of your Financial Empowerment Plan. You will maintain the overview and bring in the experts when necessary—the financial planners, the accountants, the lawyers, the tax advisors, and others. All of them ultimately are accountable to you. You should remain in control of your finances, your goals, and your overall plan. Their role is more that of copilot or assistant coach.

We help our most successful families organize and manage their teams of trusted professionals. Some already have that team in place, so we help make sure that those professionals work together to get the best results so that our clients successfully make the transition into and through a happy, successful retirement.

Over the years we have also been able to connect investors with good professional advisors from within our network, or we can help organize and manage their own advisory teams, which might consist of investment managers, accountants, insurance professionals, estate-planning attorneys, and sometimes others. Everyone will need to know what the others are doing and how their advice might impact all other facets of your overall planning. You may want someone to help you organize, manage, and keep tabs on your team of advisors and on your comprehensive Financial Empowerment Plan. And that is what we can do.

Getting to the Tough Stuff

Many families have a long way to go in their planning when they first come to see us. Couples may have talked for years about what they should do and have some general ideas, but often we find the talk has not progressed to action. In such cases, we may have to start from the beginning and help them design and implement their comprehensive Financial Empowerment Plan. We assure they have a thorough understanding of our unique and proprietary planning process and that they follow it through. One example is with estate planning: an attorney can help them to set up a trust, and we can follow up and help in funding that trust. We ensure that none of those essential steps falls through the cracks.

Sometimes we meet families that haven't considered and discussed these matters. Some couples just don't see eye to eye. Often it's just a matter of each of their preferences: the husband may be a more aggressive investor, for example, while the wife may be more conservative. Maybe she doesn't like or isn't very comfortable with an advisor they work with, who just may happen to be the husband's golf buddy from high school. Perhaps they do not agree on how their money should be divvied up to the children, grandchildren, or charities when they are gone. Sometimes just the decision to meet with us has been courageous for them.

Over the years we've experienced all these different scenarios and understand that many families often get emotional about such topics. Sometimes our role is similar to that of counselors, helping them get through tough phases in their lives. We strive to build a level of confidence and trust so they can be comfortable talking opening about their goals and planning.

We recently helped a couple, Carol and Jim, who had been having trouble communicating with each other about their retirement planning. Carol was very quiet for the first two visits, while Jim pretty much ran the show. We would try to draw out Carol's thoughts and opinions, but he consistently cut her off. During our third visit, however, we saw a shift in communication, and Carol began to lead the conversation.

"We never get around to talking about what matters," Carol said, beginning to sob as Jim sat with his arms folded. "We just fight. We've never had more than one meeting with a financial advisor because we can't get anywhere. We've met three times with you, and it's better than ever before, so we both think this is a great start to improving our marriage and our lives."

As they left our office, they told us they would be back when they had made some headway on getting along and agreeing. As we write this, they have yet to return. We are confident we made a positive impact in helping them feel more comfortable talking: expressing and understanding each other's concerns and goals. Many families experience similar communication barriers or breakdowns, some more and some less severe. Being able to help them identify and work on overcoming these concerns is quite often where our role helping them begins. The reality is some things are difficult to talk about, especially money. A big part of our job is to make sure these things do get talked about.

Relationships Founded on Trust

As fiduciary advisors we are legally required to do only what is in the client's best interest. This is the highest accountability standard in the financial industry, and it is the standard by which we must operate. A stockbroker or someone selling mutual funds or insurance may not be a legal fiduciary, meaning they only have to operate under the suitability standard and by law must only provide what is "suitable"—and that can be much different than what is in the client's best interest. Their allegiance might be more to the company they represent. Since we are fiduciary advisors, ours is strictly to the families we serve.

A fiduciary advisor must also by law disclose any and all conflicts of interest. Let's say your advisor could get a 3 percent commission to sell you Product A, or a 5 percent commission to sell you Product B. If those are comparable products, a fiduciary cannot simply sell you the second one because it offers 2 percentage points more in compensation. The fiduciary must fully disclose the method of payment and anything that is potentially in conflict with your best interest. A broker or advisor that is not held to the highest standard in the financial industry—the fiduciary standard—may have more leniency in how they disclose and get to paid to sell some investment products.

How do you know whom you are dealing with—an advisor that is held to a suitability standard or one that is held to the fiduciary standard of care? Simply ask for documentation—similar to the way you would ask contractors to verify that they are insured before letting them begin work on your house. Do some research and due diligence. Ask questions. How is this person paid, and by whom? Registered representatives working for a brokerage house are often less likely to be fiduciaries. Again, their allegiance may be more to their boss or to the firm that employs them. One of their goals may be meeting a quota or pushing a certain product so they can get a promotion, bonus, or trip, rather than making sure they are suggesting and providing what is in an investor's or family's best interest.

Have you ever noticed some professionals have an alphabet soup of letters behind their name? In the financial industry, like many others, some of these professional designations are highly credible and very difficult to obtain. However, some just show the person has taken a class, passed a test, or paid a fee, but really don't hold any water in terms of their knowledge, experience, and trustworthiness. Some designations indicate the holder is a fiduciary, but most do not.

No designation, however, guarantees that you will like the individual or whether he or she can develop a solid relationship of trust to see you through your retirement years. Bernie Madoff had credentials, and at one point he was even the Nasdaq chairman. Apparently he knew a lot about finances—and he channeled that knowledge into a multibillion-dollar Ponzi scheme. His credentials did not mean he cared about the families he was supposed to serve.

By all means, an advisor's experience, credentials, and level of education are all very important factors to consider. You should seek to work with someone who is smart and qualified and who is required by law to put your family's best interest first. Above all, though, working with someone you are comfortable with and trust is a must. One of our most successful clients told us, "Anyone can sell me services and products, but I don't trust just anyone. You've truly earned our trust and our business." It can take a while to build that kind of rapport, but it is critical. You deserve to be served by someone dedicated to your family's well-being. You need more than a product salesperson. You are in search of solutions purely in your best interest.

CHAPTER 5

WHAT'S THERE TO RISK?

SEVERAL YEARS AGO, just after the recession slammed portfolios across the country, a General Motors retiree came in to see us. His 401(k), originally about $500,000, had sunk to about $280,000.

As you can imagine, he was highly concerned. Although he and his wife had other investment accounts and some other income sources, his 401(k) was primarily how they planned to fund their retirement years, which they had just started.

"What can we do?" he asked us. "That half million was most of our life savings. We needed it to give us the income for all the things we dreamed about doing the rest of our lives. But now that's cut in half. I can't risk losing more in the market, so how can we invest what's left to give us the lifestyle we want? I'm worried we'll run out of money."

As we examined that couple's accounts, we determined that if they made some fairly simple adjustments to their current budget and investments, they wouldn't need income from his 401(k) for several years, giving their portfolio time to hopefully repair most of the damage suffered in 2008. We showed them some solutions to obtain a reasonable no-risk growth rate and restore their income level to where it needed it to be, guaranteeing their income for life without risking any more of their hard-earned dollars. Once they were comfortable with their Financial Empowerment Plan, they were able to purchase a winter home in Florida and enjoy the retirement lifestyle they had always envisioned.

Some investors whose portfolios took a beating from 2000 through 2003 and from 2008 through 2009 decided to get completely out of the market and sat on the sidelines, missing the entire recovery. Fearing the situation would worsen further, many ended up bailing out at the bottom—in other words, they sold low, when in theory they should have been buying in low. Whether unadvised or ill-advised, they lost out on an opportunity to make money.

As we have seen over the years, investors who have been hurt badly by market losses often stop thinking rationally—and that has proved to be one of the biggest investing risks of all: irrational investment decisions. Most investors naturally want to buy and own winners, not losers. When an investment is up, or the market in general is rising, they want a piece of the action. However, when investments or the markets are falling, they don't want any part of it. Even though this may be human nature, unfortunately it's also a good way to lose money. The way to make money in the stock market over time is to buy investments at a discount and sell them when they reach a higher price, not vice versa. Successful investors follow the old advice to "buy low, sell high." A good financial advisor can help investors manage their irrational emotions and overcome the cycle of fear and greed that so often steals wealth.

Market risk, however, is only one of the threats to wealth that retirees, and prospective retirees, face. A big part of our job as trusted advisors is to help manage all potential risks involved with investing. This involves helping investors design their Financial Empowerment Plans to produce a return that will meet their goals with as little risk exposure as possible, as well as dealing with such matters as inflation, taxes, fees, fluctuating interest rates, the possibility of needing some form of long-term care, and ultimately estate and legacy issues. These unfortunate risks have become increasing concerns for recent generations because people are living so much longer today than in generations past.

We will examine some of those risks in this chapter. In the chapters ahead, we will consider how to manage two of them in particular: the risk of unnecessarily paying too much in taxes and the risk that the cost of long-term care could deplete your life savings. Let's start now with a closer look at how investing in the market can make or break a portfolio.

Direct Stock Market Risk

In downturns such as the tech bubble burst of 2000–2003 and the financial crisis of 2008–2009, many investors saw how a fairly substantial nest egg can be depleted if it is overexposed to risky investments. These are times when investors learn the real meanings of "average annual return" and "volatility." Investors don't need to be experts in finance to understand and see how these two concepts can affect their investments, standards of living, and retirement dreams.

Let's take a look at two portfolios that each averaged the exact same rate of return, 5.67 percent, over the same ten years. The first portfolio took an extremely volatile path to get there. One year it was up 50 percent, and the next it was down 50 percent. The other portfolio had a much smoother ride, a lot less volatility, with the percentages of gains and losses being considerably smaller. Ironically, the end result was that both portfolios had the exact same average annual return. With higher volatility, it's actually possible to have the same or even lower annual average return but end up with more money. If you're anything like most of the families we work with, having more money is probably more important than your average returns.

How does higher volatility impact your income? Let's say that each of those investors was withdrawing an income every year of 5 percent of their totals. Even though their annual average returns over the same time frame were the same, based on the lower or higher volatility of each portfolio, their amount of income and overall portfolio values would be drastically different. The more an investment declines with higher volatility, compounded with the income taken out, the less money it will yield. The math shows that if you lose 35 percent of an investment, you will need a return of 53.85 percent just to break even. And if you happen to be taking out an additional 5 percent for income, you will need 66.67 percent just to break even.

In our experience this is why it is so important to adopt a disciplined, low-volatility approach to investing. In your retirement years, you may need to rely on your life savings to produce a lifelong income. Your financial plan must be flexible enough to handle all your needs and still be able to recover efficiently when troubles strike. Your Financial Empowerment Plan should be built to weather all storms.

Wall Street—the stock market—by design is driven by growth and the opportunity to make money. The growth times in the market are referred to as "bulls," and the losing times are referred to as "bears." If you visit the New York Stock Exchange, you will see a big statue by the entrance of a charging bull. What you won't find is a statue of a bear. Most investors, however, know that the market is not always bullish, it doesn't always go up, and the bear comes lumbering in regularly, but Wall Street only wants to see that bull. The careers of stockbrokers and mutual fund managers are built on growth, growth, growth.

A well-diversified and disciplined investment approach, however, needs to be built for any economic scenario. Both the bull and the bear can come to the market every day, every month, every quarter. Your investment discipline should not be built around the all-bull mentality of Wall Street. It should also be prepared for the bears that are sure to visit. Many of today's investors have lived through many years when the market seemed to rise endlessly. Only since the turn of the millennium have investors seen bigger corrections. Many investors tend to lose sight of the unfortunate negative situation that can happen. They expect that only all-time new market highs will continue.

Your financial plan must be flexible enough to handle all your needs and still be able to recover efficiently when troubles strike. Your Financial Empowerment Plan should be built to weather all storms.

A good advisor's job is to watch for those inevitable downturns, looking for ways to minimize the threats of losses, perhaps reallocating some money into safer investments rather than sticking with the swing-for-the-fence, growth-at-all-costs approach. A growth-oriented broker who isn't focused on managing downside risk might tell you to just wait, hang in there, that the market will come back— even if it might take several years. A lower volatility risk-management philosophy seeks to minimize the loss and maintain the growth so that you don't find yourself in retirement and losing a substantial amount of your portfolio—and then what?

The goal should be to hang on to your gains, not to just hang on for the ride. "You guys taught us the simplest rule about investing," one of our clients told us. "If we don't lose so much when the market goes down, we don't have to be so aggressive and try to make so much when it comes back." Research has shown that low volatility is what consistently wins the race over the long term. The level of volatility is what will make you or break you as an investor. In building and managing Financial Empowerment Plans, we don't just look for the highest average return over the course of time, we look out for the volatility potential as well. We look for investments that will earn you a reasonable rate of return while taking on the least amount of risk. In other words, we aim to help you achieve your financial goals with the highest probability of success.

A good way to understand volatility is to visualize two paths to the same destination: one path with bigger ups and downs, and the other path with smaller ups and downs. The first path, you might say, would be rougher than the second path. Now think about the investment journey of your money: Do you want the rougher or smoother ride to achieving your goals?

When you experience a loss in your portfolio, you also experience the lost opportunity of the potential growth on the money you lost. If you lose $50,000, for instance, had you kept that money in your portfolio and earned a 7 percent return over twenty years, that $50,000 would have grown to over $193,000. That is your real loss, or what we call "negative compounding of losing money." As Warren Buffett explained, "Rule number one is never lose money. Rule number two is never forget rule number one."

Don't Lose Your Financial Balance

A question we get asked quite often when we help families with their Financial Empowerment Plan is "How much of our money should we have in riskier investments, and how much should we have in safer, principal-protected ones?" A simple rule of thumb or guide that we often use to help investors with how much of their money should be invested in riskier and how much in safer investments is known as the "Rule of 100," which comes from John Bogle, the founder of The Vanguard Group. This really is just a simple rule of thumb to use as a starting point for how much of a portfolio should be invested in stocks or equity-type investments, which tend to have more upside potential and bear more downside risk, and how much should be invested in bonds or other fixed-income type investments, which tend to have less upside but also less downside potential. The Rule of 100 suggests that you subtract your age from 100, and the resulting figure is the percentage of your portfolio that would make good financial sense to invest in riskier investments. The rest of your money should be invested in fixed-income alternatives, or safer investments. That formula is designed to build a portfolio that becomes increasingly less aggressive, with less risk of losing money as you move into and through retirement. As a guideline, the Rule of 100 is a good place to start for families seeking to achieve their retirement goals, and some have even started using 120 rather than 100.

When we ask families if the Rule of 100 looks and sounds good for their money, quite often they tell us that's still a little too risky. Looking at how their portfolios are invested when they first come to see us, however, we often see their actual risk level is the opposite of what the formula would recommend, even riskier than they are comfortable with. For example, the Rule of 100 would suggest that a sixty-year-old should have about 40 percent of his or her portfolio in riskier investments and 60 percent in safer investments. However, a heavier allocation to riskier investments like the 80 percent in portfolio B would result in much higher risk and the potential of losing a greater amount of wealth than portfolio A, which is allocated as the Rule of 100 suggests.

Of course, there are a lot of other factors and variables that ultimately go into determining the appropriate balance of a family's portfolio. Each family's particular needs and circumstances must be factored into an overall investment strategy that makes sense. Over the years we have also worked with many investors who, despite what the Rule of 100 might indicate, are comfortable with a much higher percentage of their money invested in more growth-oriented or riskier investments. One thing we've learned in helping so many families over the years is that every investor/family is different, and each has their own comfort zone for accepting risk. Often, though, families are surprised to learn that they actually face more risk of loss than they thought they did before working with us. We help them design a plan that reduces their overall risk exposure to a level that they are more comfortable with and that meets their goals and lifestyle requirements.

Once we have established the appropriate risk level and investment balance within an investor's portfolio, it's important to keep an eye on it and manage it over time. As time goes by, the amount of money originally invested in each sector, category, and investment will likely change with ongoing market and interest rate fluctuations. This is the process of rebalancing, which ensures a portfolio stays in line with its overall goals and objectives.

For most people, this process of rebalancing their portfolio may not come naturally. Rebalancing requires an investment discipline based on math, and most importantly one that doesn't become overrun by emotions. Possibly one of the oldest concepts relating to how to make money in stocks or the stock market is to "buy low, sell high." Actually doing this—selling off winners that have some nice gains and buying losers that are down in value—is a struggle and often difficult for investors to do. This is where having a disciplined investment plan based on algorithms and math helps remove the emotional biases that so often hinder investors from maximizing their financial opportunities of capturing gains when investments are up and taking advantage of discounted buying opportunities of investments that are down but still offer good upside potential.

Another philosophy in investing, known as "buy and hold," is much more passive and tends to ignore the potential need for more active rebalancing. This philosophy tells investors to hang in there and wait it out, as eventually it'll come back. When families come in to meet with us, we ask them to describe to us what their current or previous advisor was telling them to do during the market downturn of 2008–2009. One of the most common, and unfortunate, responses we hear over and over is that their advisors just kept telling them to "hang in there; just wait; it'll come back." In other words, their advisors were being more passive, less active, and didn't have any downside protection plan other than to do nothing.

Let's think about this "do nothing" philosophy outside of your money: when driving down the highway, do you keep up the same speed, no matter what might happen? If you were cruising along at seventy miles an hour on a sunny afternoon and all of a sudden the sky turned black and it started to pour, chances are you would probably slow down a little bit—if not a lot—or maybe even pull over to wait out the storm. This is similar to how we believe your portfolio should be actively managed. When you're experiencing or see trouble ahead, you should back off on the throttle and proceed with more caution. Adjusting how you invest during volatile times just makes good financial sense to us and the families we serve, as no one wants to miss out on their goals due to a financial crash.

Inflation Risk

With inflation so low for so long, many families haven't thought about it much. If you are retired or getting near that age, you might remember when inflation was a double-digit nightmare. However, even at a steady, low rate, inflation can still erode away at our money and buying power over time. To buy something that would have cost a dollar in 1986, you would need well over two dollars today. When it comes to income, if you earn $100,000 a year today, you will need over $180,000 in income in twenty years to get the same buying power if inflation averages 3 percent over those years

Inflation is one of those outside factors that we as investors cannot control. We can, however, control the strategies and tools we use in our approach to the potential moves of the markets and inflation. A lot of families have told us they want to make sure their investment return at least stays a few percentage points ahead of inflation. If the inflation rate is 3 percent and your return on investments is only 2 percent, you will ultimately be losing portfolio value and purchasing power due to inflation risk. In several years you will notice that your dollars don't buy as much. It is often true that we should invest less aggressively and more conservatively in retirement, but if we invest too conservatively, inflation could take a negative toll on our portfolios. We need to be aware of inflation and the return on our investments to try to find a successful balance.

Every family is different when it comes to how much return above inflation they need to achieve. Some investors don't need their portfolio for immediate income, but rather as a means of growth to stay ahead of inflation over time. Other families rely on their portfolio to provide income to maintain their daily lifestyles. It is important to identify which is the case for you so your hard-earned money can be invested accordingly. Our role as trusted fiduciary advisors is to help our families build and manage low-volatility plans that give them the highest probability of retirement success, which includes staying ahead of inflation and maintaining or even increasing their purchasing power.

Interest Rate Risk

Retirees also run the risk that higher interest rates they may have experienced in the past may not be what they receive in the future. Not long ago certificates of deposit (CDs) had annual yields from 5 to 7 percent. If you had based your retirement goals on expecting a CD return in that range, where would you be now, with the minuscule rates we have been seeing in recent years? Unfortunately, as of the time of writing, with interest rates at all-time lows, CDs have really just become certificates of depreciation.

If you had $1 million in CDs when the return was 6 percent, you might have felt comfortable with the $60,000-a-year yield you were getting. However, we have met many families that saw their rate drop by as much as 4 percentage points or more when those CDs matured and it was time to reinvest in new ones. A 2 percent return on a million dollars is only $20,000 a year, and dipping into the principal to make up the difference only reduces future earnings even further. As investors we all hope that rates will rise again sometime soon, but we can't count on it. In fact, many argue that CD rates will never rise to a level that will support a comfortable retirement like they once did with double-digit returns.

Bond investors should also pay close attention to interest rate risk. As interest rates rise, the value of bonds will fall—this is a formula known as duration. Think of a teeter-totter, with the value of bonds at one end and interest rates at the other. As one goes up, the other goes down, as they work in inverse relation to each other. As interest rates were on a steady decline since the mid-1980s, in turn bond yields were on the rise. The Federal Reserve has often raised interest rates when it feels the need to keep the economy from overheating, just as it lowers rates to stimulate the economy. Investors who purchase bonds in a low-interest-rate environment run a greater risk that interest rates will rise—and the value and/or yield of those bonds will decrease, which is known as interest rate risk.

When you expect interest rates will go up, such as when they are at historical lows, you shouldn't invest in these types of bonds/fixed-income securities that will produce a lower yield as interest rates rise. You run the risk that your fixed rate will be surpassed by what is available for other investments and that your portfolio could therefore lose value or additional buying power.

When interest rates rise or fall, the duration of a particular fixed-income investment can be used to calculate how much its yield will change. The longer the term of the bond, the more its value will rise or fall. Think of the teeter-totter. If you are sitting at the end of the board, you will rise higher and fall lower. If you sit closer to the center, your rise and fall will be shorter. When rates rise, bonds with longer durations will potentially suffer a greater loss in value than bonds with shorter durations.

Once again, don't keep driving the car at the same speed regardless of conditions. As we write this, interest rates appear to be at all-time lows, with some even in negative territory. Historically, investors who want to reduce their market risk have put money in more conservative fixed-income investments such as bonds, or retail bond mutual funds. In a climate of rising interest rates, however, does it make good financial sense to invest in something that is likely to experience a loss in value?

In the fixed-income world, bonds are just one of many different investment options. Some work in this inverse relation to interest rates, while others actually work in direct relation with interest rates, meaning their values and yields will rise or fall in the same direction as the rates. As interest rates rise, their values will rise, and vice versa. When we build Financial Empowerment Plans for families, we try to use investments that have the best chance to go up in value over time. When interest rates are rising, investment options with that direct relationship make more financial sense. When the rates start to go back down, that is the time to rebalance and readjust your portfolio, looking once again to use those investments that move in inverse relation to falling interest rates.

The Risk of Fees

One of our best clients has a simple and logical explanation of fees: "A fee is something you pay, and value is what you receive." He told us early on in our relationship that the fees he paid were more than justified by the "over-the-top" value he received.

As fee-based advisors, we, too, believe it is okay to pay a fee—after all, nothing good in life is free. However, it is vital to the overall success of your portfolio to understand all your fees and what they do to your bottom line.

In our experience, a lot of investors are unaware how much their portfolio can be drained by fees that they might not even know exist. Some investments that may have fees are mutual funds, different types of annuities, index funds, and ETFs, just to name a few. Let's take a look at some of the investment fees typically charged in the mutual funds that make up a large portion of so many investment portfolios today.

A typical retail mutual fund could have at least three fees: the fund manager's annual fee, annual internal trading fees known as "turnover," the broker's sales commission, or maybe even an advisor fee. Mutual funds are in a way categorized by how much and when the investors will pay commissions. These commissions are generally deducted from the investor's account, either up front when the fund is purchased (A-share funds), ongoing annually (C-share funds), or upon sale of the fund within a certain time frame (B-share funds). We have seen these commissions range from 3 to 5.75 percent. The broker may also charge a wrap fee, usually a flat percentage of all the assets under his or her management. Not including commissions, it is not unusual to see mutual fund fees in the 1.5 to 3 percent range per year.

If the annual mutual fund fee is 3 percent and the fund grows 5 percent in a year, the investor might see only 2 percent actual net growth. If the fund loses 10 percent in a bad year, the investor actually experiences a 13 percent loss. As you can see, fees can significantly influence the net results of a portfolio, particularly over the long haul.

The Securities and Exchange Commission requires that all mutual fund companies produce and distribute a prospectus. The prospectus must disclose all the fund's possible charges, risks, objectives, conflicts of interest, and more. The fund company must mail a prospectus annually to each shareholder who buys the fund for as long as he or she owns the fund. Many investors never read the prospectus, but it does contain essential information.

The fee section of the prospectus incudes a box or diagram that discloses the commissions and the annual management fee, or

12b-1 fees. Below that diagram are often disclaimers, one of which references the fund's turnover and applicable fees. Turnover is the fund manager's purchase or sale of individual holdings within the fund. Usually, within the next few pages of the prospectus is a section disclosing that the fund imposes fees and commissions when it turns over holdings and that these fees are in addition to the annual management fee.

A variety of other expenses can add to the true cost of owning a mutual fund. Consider what that means for your money. Unfortunately, many investors have expressed to us that such details about all of fees involved in owning mutual funds were not fully disclosed or discussed prior to the purchase and or even after the purchase of their funds.

When you do receive a mutual fund prospectus, we highly encourage you to spend some time trying to read through it and get a better understanding of what you own, and don't ever feel shy or embarrassed to ask the person that sold you the fund to help better explain the things you may not fully understand. You need to know what it all means, particularly as it relates to your investment objectives, the rate of return you are trying to get, the fees you are comfortable with paying, and the amount of risk and potential loss you are willing to accept.

As fiduciary advisors we feel it is important for investors to understand all their options when considering how to invest, including their choices of mutual funds—especially the charges, fees, and commissions they may end up paying. We are fee-based advisors, which means we get paid an agreed-upon annual flat fee from the families we work for. We do not charge any commissions on mutual fund purchases. In today's industry, mutual funds are primarily sold by commission-driven brokers. Nothing is inherently wrong with that.

Commissions are just another way to pay for an investment and the advice and management you hope to receive.

The four most common ways a mutual fund is sold are as A-share, B-share, C-share, and no-load or institutional share. These options all apply to the same fund and are invested and managed the same way, and with the same annual performance before fees, no matter which share class you own. The difference is in the nature and timing of the commission paid to the broker or to the retail shop. The annual management fees also will vary, which all have a negative impact on the actual net return the investors receive.

- With an A-share (or "front-load") mutual fund, you pay the commission up front. If it is 5 percent and you invest $10,000, the broker takes his or her commission out of your money, and you will have $9,500 working for you on day one. We had a new client tell us that when he had to pay that front-load commission to a broker out of his initial investment, it was like starting out with a 5 percent loss. It didn't make good financial sense to him; nor does it to us.

- With a B-share (or "back-end load") mutual fund, you pay no commission up front. In a way, it works like a CD. If it has a five-year maturity and you sell it within that time, you will pay a commission when you sell it. If you wait until after the maturity date to sell the fund, you pay no commission. That would seem to make sense for buy-and-hold investors, but what we have found over the years is that such investors still usually get sold mutual funds that pay the commission up front. Another client mentioned to us that during the two decades when he worked with a big-box broker-dealer firm, his broker always sold him A-share funds. After learning about the other options, the client told us he felt his broker was looking out for his own interest more, making sure he wouldn't lose his commissions by getting paid up front on the initial investment.

- With a C-share mutual fund, which some have said is the most expensive type of mutual fund to own, you do not pay a commission at the time of buying or selling the fund. Instead, you pay a continuing "level load" of up to 1 percent every year, whether or not anything is bought or sold. This C-share commission is added to the annual management expense of the fund, which could push the overall annual fees into the 2 to 3 percent range or higher.

- With an institutional share (or "no-load") mutual fund, you pay no commission, either up front or at the back. This is the only type of mutual fund that we would want the families we help to own—presuming, that is, that mutual funds make the best financial sense in their portfolios.

Another consideration when choosing a mutual fund is that the annual management fee may be different based on the share class of the fund you purchase. The no-load institutional class generally has the lowest annual management fee. In other words, whenever you pay a commission to buy a fund, it's also common to get hit with a higher annual management fee. The annual management fee generally will not be quite as high if you pay the commission up front for an A-share. If you buy a B-share—which, again, is the exact same fund, managed exactly the same way, with the same annual performance before fees—you may be charged a higher annual management fee, resulting in a net lower return, for the privilege of not having to pay the commission up front.

Another "interesting" part of the financial industry and the relationship between mutual fund manufacturers and the companies that sell the funds is the practice of revenue sharing. Revenue sharing is a financial relationship regarding how much of a mutual fund's annual fees the mutual fund company will share with the company that sold the funds. Revenue sharing happens in a lot of industries—like the automotive and pharmaceutical fields, for example. Sometimes it is referred to as a kickback, and it amounts to this: "If you sell our products, we will give you a cut of the profits. If you sell even more, we will kick back even more."

Over the years, when families have brought their investment statements in for us to run their current holdings through our proprietary Portfolio Stress Test and Second Opinion, we have identified patterns that show they own a lot of the same company's mutual funds. One couple asked us during their initial visit why twelve of the fifteen funds that their broker had sold them were from the same company. Our analysis and research discovered that that particular mutual fund company paid the broker's employer the highest percentage of revenue sharing, or kickback, for selling all their funds. The broker's employers' website generally discloses these revenue sharing conflicts of interest, but in our experience they are not very easy to find. For this company, their revenue sharing disclosure was buried multiple pages deep under miscellaneous tabs. When we printed the disclosure and showed it to the couple, as I am sure you can imagine, they were upset. All these years, they said, they had thought their broker was looking out for their best interests, not for his own interest or his company's profits, which they said they now didn't believe had been the case.

As fiduciary advisors, by law, we must fully disclose any and all fees an investor could be charged based on his or her portfolio and investments that we will help manage, and we must disclose and discuss any potential conflicts of interest we might have. We are required by law to have these conversations and provide any and all supporting documents to our clients before they engage with us and buy anything—*before*, not after, as well as on an ongoing annual basis. We must put your best interest first, not our own or anyone else's.

The Biggest Risk of All

We have given you an overview of many of the risks to your wealth that you need to consider when planning your retirement. As you turn the pages deeper into this book, you will read about other threats to your wealth, such as taxation and the cost of long-term care. These, too, if not carefully managed, could diminish your investments, income, and retirement dreams.

Close attention to such details has become particularly important as our life spans have lengthened. When people lived only a few years into retirement, if they reached retirement at all, they didn't worry as much about earning enough return on their money to give them sufficient income for many more years. They simply did not require a portfolio with enough punch to get them through decades of elderly unemployment. They figured their pension and Social Security would suffice.

Now, in the 401(k) era, many folks maintain that mindset. Then, when retirement suddenly is on their radar, they fear they will fall short, which can lead them to make big mistakes. Trying to catch up, they shoot for higher gains, taking on too much risk, potentially making a bad situation worse. They may end up overdrawing their accounts as they try to continue a lifestyle they no longer can support. They let fear get the better of them.

Others aim for returns higher than they need to support a comfortable lifestyle. In effect, they gamble with their life savings. They, too, are taking on excessive risk that could wreck their retirement dreams, but it isn't fear that is motivating them to do so. They are letting greed get the better of them.

The biggest threat to retirement success, in other words, often lies within the human head and heart. In our experience over the years, through good times and bad, portfolios tend to fall apart when investors let their emotions and personal biases and philosophies rule their decisions. Retirement planning must be done rationally. We educate families to understand that if they plan properly, start early, take all the right steps, and follow a disciplined investment approach, they will have a far better chance of achieving financial success and peace of mind in retirement.

> **Portfolios tend to fall apart when investors let their emotions and personal biases and philosophies rule their decisions. Retirement planning must be done rationally.**

CHAPTER 6

TAMING THE TAXES

"WE HAVE ACHIEVED our retirement goal of having over a million dollars saved in our investment portfolio," the couple told us, "and we're all set for retirement—but we're not done yet! We figure this is a good time to partner with our daughter. She's a landlord in Oregon."

This was a conversation we had with one of our successful families as we helped them build their version of a Financial Empowerment Plan. They wanted to buy a rental building with their daughter, and they figured they could use about $500,000 of their savings for that purpose.

"Do you realize," we asked them, "that the million dollars in your portfolio is not all yours?" Most of their investments had been growing over the years inside their IRA and 401(k) accounts, we explained, so all that money would be subject to ordinary income tax when they took it out. "After you pay the IRS their share in taxes," we pointed out, "you are likely to only have about $300,000 to $400,000 left."

To some this might seem obvious, but until visiting with us, this couple had not thought of it that way and taken the reality of taxes into consideration. They had always thought if they saved, invested, and grew their portfolio to their million-dollar goal, they would be financially secure and able to live the lifestyle they wanted. After further discussion, they were saddened to realize that if they proceeded with their investment idea with their daughter and paid the taxes due, they would have only a few hundred thousand dollars remaining in their retirement fund.

"Wow. We would have to pay that much in taxes to the IRS?" they asked.

"That's right. You did a wonderful job saving, investing, and growing the money inside your IRAs and 401(k)s, but those are all tax-deferred accounts. When you take the money out, the taxes you saved on all those years becomes due. The government is going to want its full cut."

That put a damper on their business venture with the daughter. Had they set aside some of their money over the years in a tax-free investment, such as a Roth IRA, they could have pulled money out of that account without having to share any of their money with the IRS. But their accounts were fully taxable, which stopped them in their tracks. Other people may want to unload an investment property to fund their retirement, and they, too, can encounter a staggering tax bill that gives them second thoughts about how to proceed.

As you can see, taxation considerations make up a big part of a comprehensive implementation of your Financial Empowerment Plan. During their years of contributing to a 401(k) or IRA type of retirement plan, investors get used to getting tax deductions for their contributions and deferral on all their growth. Tax-deferred growth is quite a beneficial arrangement and helps immensely during the accumulation-of-wealth phase of life. However, in retirement, when investors decide to start taking income from their accounts, the landscape and rules change. Once they begin to withdraw that money, all those taxes start to come due. The benefit of tax-deferred growth can feel more like a tax penalty when taking income from tax-deferred accounts, especially once investors hit their early seventies and are forced by the IRS to take money out of their accounts every year for the rest of their lives.

We have worked with a lot of retirees in that situation who need an advisor familiar with the financial patterns of the retirement stage of life. Your tax risk does not necessarily mean that some major mistake or unanticipated circumstance will sweep away much of your portfolio. Often, taxes get paid unnecessarily in dribs and drabs, a little falling through the cracks each year but adding up to a significant sum. Good tax management can protect you against such unfortunate tax oversights.

Taxable, Tax-Deferred, and Tax-Free

A solid wealth management plan for retirement should include three kinds of investment accounts—taxable, tax-deferred, and tax-free. How these three types of accounts are managed, and how and when you pull income from them could make all the difference in a tax-efficient, awesome retirement.

Taxable investments are those in which you pay the taxes in the same year that they produce gains for you, whether you take out income or not. The gains on your investments inside these accounts are taxed as either interest or dividend income, or short-term or long-term capital gains, which could be lower, higher, or the same tax percentage as your income tax and are determined by how long you own the investment before you sell it.

The interest or gains inside of tax-deferred investments, on the other hand, are not taxed in the year they are made, but rather in the year which you take money out. The most common types of tax-deferred accounts are your employer-sponsored plans like 401(k)s, 403(b)s, 457s, and others, as well as IRAs. When you invest in these accounts, you get a tax deduction for the amounts that you contribute for that tax year, and over the years, the taxes on any and all gains inside the accounts are not due, but rather deferred or kicked down the road, until you take money out. Any money that is withdrawn from tax-deferred accounts is considered ordinary income on that year's tax return.

Tax-free investments by their favorable tax treatment alone are appealing and in our experience worth looking into if they would be in your best interest. Roth IRAs, cash value of properly structured life insurance, HSAs, some college savings plans, and municipal bonds are really the only types of tax-free accounts allowed under our current United States Income Tax Code. The Roth IRA, the most common for today's investors, was established by Congress as part of the Taxpayer Relief Act of 1997 and was named for its chief sponsor, Senator William Roth of Delaware. Unlike in a traditional IRA, you do not get a tax deduction for the amount that you contribute to a Roth IRA. However, when you withdraw the money during retirement, 100 percent of that money—everything you put in plus all of the gains—is not taxed. No interest/dividend taxes, no short-term/long-term capital gains taxes, and no state or federal income taxes. Under today's tax laws, all of the earnings and income from your Roth IRA are 100 percent tax free! This tax-free aspect again makes the Roth IRA a very appealing and potentially powerful type of investment to own in your portfolio.

Having money in all three of these types of accounts—taxable, tax-deferred and tax-free—could allow you to be able to have a higher income in retirement, yet a lower taxable income, ultimately resulting in you receiving more income and paying less in taxes. If you withdrew $100,000 from your portfolio, for example, and all of the income came from a tax-deferred account, as a married couple under 2020 tax laws, you would be in the 12 percent federal income taxes bracket. However, if you had been investing in tax-free accounts as well and you pulled $50,000 out of each tax-deferred and tax-free accounts, you could potentially only be in the 10 percent or even 0 percent federal income tax bracket. Depending on your tax bracket, you could even pay long-term capital gains as low as 0–15 percent on earnings from taxable accounts, which could ultimately be lower than the taxes you would pay on ordinary income. Again, this could be a very powerful, tax-efficient strategy for your retirement income—less in taxes could mean more in your pocket.

With an employer-sponsored plan like a 401(k)/403(b), your employer might also offer to match a percentage of your contributions. Any form of company match is a great deal—it's like free money, and we strongly advise anyone who has such a benefit to take full advantage of it. As nice as tax-deferred accounts are, it is important that you recognize that, like the couple in our opening story, you eventually must pay that deferred tax. You will be taxed on everything that you and your employer contributed, plus all of the growth, at whatever tax bracket you will be in when you take out money for income.

A potential downside to a 401(k) or similar employer-sponsored plan is that your employer gets to pick the custodian of your money and the menu of investment options you have to choose from. In our experience of seeing hundreds of different employer-sponsored plans over the years, such plans don't usually offer a quantity or quality of fund choices in the employee's best interest, especially for those approaching and into retirement. For investors who have the opportunity, it may be more beneficial to roll your money over into your own self-directed IRA if you have the in-service rollover option available with your employer while you are still working, or as soon as you can after you retire.

Nonetheless, the 401(k)-type plans, known as defined contribution, have become a very popular benefit provided by employers, and they are replacing the traditional employer pensions, known as defined-benefit plans. With this shift and the increased popularity of 401(k)-type plans, there are currently trillions of dollars tucked away in these types of tax-deferred accounts. The government certainly will be eager to stake its tax claim on that huge resource. It is not a given that your tax rate will be lower during retirement. These plans are helping a vast number of people save for their futures, but they must be careful that they do not defer their taxes into a potential tax mess later in life. We cannot control how the rates or the brackets might change. What we can do, however, is plan accordingly and use the most tax-efficient investment vehicles regardless of what is happening economically and politically.

In recent years some employers who offer 401(k) plans have been adding Roth accounts as an option. This can be a highly advantageous way for people to begin building a tax-free option, as well as a tax-deferred account, so that they might be able to withdraw their money as tax efficiently as possible during retirement. The money that an employee contributes to a Roth, of course, would not be eligible for a deduction off of that year's income, but it could grow to a huge benefit for the retirement years. Some employers are also offering guaranteed lifetime annuities inside the 401(k) plan so that participants can design their own personal pension, which could be another very powerful benefit for those that don't have an employer-sponsored guaranteed lifetime pension.

If your employer does offer a Roth 401(k) option, you can contribute much more than you would be allowed to put into a Roth IRA outside of an employer plan. As of 2020 the IRS limits contributions into a Roth IRA to only $7,000 for those under fifty, although that limit is increased to $7,000 if you are fifty or over. However, with a Roth 401(k), you can contribute $19,000 a year, or $25,000 if you are fifty or over.

Converting to a Roth

There's a pretty good chance that even before reading this book, you had heard of a Roth IRA, and for good reason. The Roth IRA was introduced by Senator Roth in 1997, and by law as of this writing, Roth IRAs allow all gains inside the Roth to grow tax free and for all the income/distributions taken from the Roth IRA to be free from any and all taxes as well. The money you deposit/convert into a Roth IRA will have already been taxed—from there on out, Roth IRAs are 100 percent income and capital gains *tax free*. Because of these tax-free features, investors have been contributing and converting to Roth IRAs very aggressively since the Roth was introduced.

We have helped a lot of families not only contribute to Roth IRAs but also convert their 401(k) plans and their traditional IRAs into Roth IRAs. Any amount you convert from a tax-deferred account to a tax-free Roth IRA you must include as ordinary income on your tax return for the year you convert the funds. It is important to identify and understand what the tax bill will be before making such conversions. Such conversions could potentially increase your income tax rate for that year, as well as potentially affect the taxation of your Social Security benefits and your Medicare premiums.

By converting money out of your tax-deferred accounts and paying some of that tax bill up front, you will also reduce the amount that you will be forced to withdraw from these accounts as a required minimum distribution every year starting in your seventies, because there is no such thing as government-forced required minimum distributions from Roth IRAs. It is very possible that you will not need as much income in your seventies, eighties, and even nineties, as Uncle Sam will insist that you withdraw every year for the rest of your life. By reducing the amount of money you have in tax-deferred accounts and increasing the amount in your tax-free Roth IRA, you in effect will be biting smaller tax bullets annually along the way to avoid being financially blown up by a potentially much bigger tax bomb later.

Like most of the best things in life, the longer you can experience the benefits, the better off you'll be. The younger you are when you start contributing and/or converting to Roth IRAs, the longer time you'll hopefully have to reap the tax-free growth. However, when investors are in their sixties, seventies, and even eighties, we have been able to help a lot of them benefit from Roth conversions for tax-free growth, income, and wealth transfer, especially with the current lower tax brackets of the Tax Cuts and Jobs Act of 2017. The million-dollar questions we get asked every day might be going through your mind as you read this: Should we convert our 401(k)s and IRAs to Roth IRAs, and how much should we convert? Ultimately, what makes the most financial sense will depend on a lot of current and future variables for you and your family, and we can't stress enough that every family is different.

If they will consider a Roth IRA for tax-free income, another way we've helped a large number of families to manage their current and future tax liabilities and receive tax-free income in retirement is to draw money out of the cash value of a life insurance policy. We're not talking about the traditional, old version of death benefit life insurance, or term insurance, where you want to pay the least amount of premium for the greatest death benefit you can get in case you die with debt or obligations to cover for your spouse, but rather an advanced planning concept called LIRP (life insurance for retirement planning). We help families utilize these vehicles as an alternative asset class for some of their safer money, to provide tax-free income, tax-free access to the death benefit should they need long-term care, and, of course, a pretty nice amount of tax-free money for wealth transfer as well. Again, what is in the best interest of each investor/family ultimately depends on each investor's/family's unique situation.

When considering doing IRA-to-Roth-IRA conversion, be sure you are aware of and understand the different "five-year rules," which depend on how old you are when you make the conversions. Also remember that any amount you withdraw, or convert, out of a tax-deferred account will be taxed as ordinary income in the year of the transaction. You can choose to pay the taxes due out of the amount withdrawn/converted; however, this will reduce the amount going into your new investment, so it might make better financial sense to pay the taxes due from other already taxed sources if you can. If you are younger than 59½ years old, you definitely don't want to use your IRA money to pay the taxes, as you will incur a 10 percent early withdrawal penalty from the IRS, on top of the taxes owed.

Let the Buyer Beware

During your accumulation years, as you invest money year after year into your 401(k) or other employer-sponsored plans, you don't often hear much about the potential future tax liabilities growing inside your accounts. Most advisors and investors who are in the accumulation phase of life tend to focus more on saving taxes one year at a time and getting as much tax-deferred growth within the accounts as possible, with the mindset of "Don't worry about the taxes until you need the money." Unfortunately, this potentially large tax liability becomes a stark reality when investors shift into the preservation and distribution phase of their lives in retirement, and especially when forced to take required minimum distributions by the IRS.

You and your advisor need to structure a plan to reduce your current and future tax liabilities into and through retirement as much as possible.

Seeing as you received a tax deduction for every dollar you invested into your 401(k), and those dollars have been growing without any annual taxation, the reality is you must expect that you will pay your fair share of taxes. However, with proper knowledge and guidance regarding the current tax laws, you may be able to have a say in the matter of reducing and minimizing the amount of your fair share. That calls for knowledge and action. You and your advisor need to structure a plan to reduce your current and future tax liabilities into and through retirement as much as possible. It is important to us as fiduciary advisors to help educate investors about the potential future tax liabilities they might be adding as they make annual contributions into tax-deferred accounts. Being educated and aware can help you make better-informed decisions into and through a more tax-efficient retirement.

CHAPTER 7

WHEN ILLNESS STRIKES

THE LOVING COUPLE FELT young and vibrant at age sixty and were looking forward to enjoying many carefree years of retirement together. The husband had long provided his family with a decent living with his job at General Motors while his wife managed the home front, doing what she loved most—taking care of her family.

When he was sixty-two, however, he was diagnosed with cancer and forced to retire. He lived twelve more years while his wife cared for him in their home. When he died, she was left to carry on as best she could. Her income consisted only of his Social Security widow's benefit—none of her own—and not much of his pension to live on. Despite his cancer, he had chosen a pension option that left much less to her in exchange for more money for the two of them while he was alive. She was all right for a few years, but then her own health failed. She went into a nursing home for a while, then spent her final months living with one of her daughters four states away from her other children.

This couple could have used some good financial advice much earlier in their lives. They had a broker who bought and sold stocks for them and otherwise were what we call "do-it-themselfers." They did not have a fiduciary advisor looking out for them. No one was helping them with their tax planning, pension decisions, longevity income planning, asset protection, or long-term care insurance.

That story is very personal to us. For one of us, it is the story of Mom and Dad; for the other, it is the story of Grandma and Grandpa. This experience in our own family had a lot to do with why we got into this business and why we are writing this book.

A Major Risk to Your Wealth—Your Health

Over the years we have met many couples like my grandma and grandpa. As they approach retirement, they don't often think about what might happen to their lifestyle and finances if they experience serious health issues. Many retirees live a retirement free of serious health concerns; however, the longer we are living, the more susceptible we could become to our health declining—"Ah, the joys of getting old."

Medical advancements also add to the possibility of a longer life and more years to enjoy retirement—or, sometimes, this can mean living longer with lingering health issues. A serious question we believe everyone should consider and prepare for is what happens if your health begins to decline and you get to the point where you need constant care, or if that happens to your spouse? That would obviously present a multitude of challenges; one such potential problem is the added pressure on your retirement portfolio to pay for different forms of healthcare. Some people fear their investments and savings could be spent down and drained a lot faster than they had planned and would have wanted due to the unfortunate and potentially high healthcare costs in retirement.

In our experience a lot of savers and investors do not accurately anticipate the out-of-pocket costs they could face from medical expenses and long-term care in the event their health declines. Some actually believe that Medicare will cover everything for them, including the costs of long-term care. They are in for a big disappointment if they believe that. Others have told us that they will just go on the state's program and Medicaid will take care of them. The reality is that those two taxpayer-funded programs, Medicare and Medicaid, are far from a good solution should your health, or your spouse's health, decline. For one thing, Medicare is very limited, paying only for the first hundred days in a government-approved facility, and only if admission to the long-term care facility is directly from a hospital.

Medicaid has sometimes been referred to as a forced poverty program. If you fail to plan properly for covering such medical costs and as a result go broke, then you may qualify for Medicaid, when in reality you might not want to. Long-term care facilities that serve Medicaid patients generally receive less compensation, and that tends to be reflected in the quality of the facility and the care provided. In our experience, most of the families we have met who have had a family member on Medicaid tell us they wish that wasn't so.

Long-Term Care Insurance and Alternatives

Long-term care insurance (LTCI) is not health insurance as some may think of it. A better way to think about LTCI is wealth-protection insurance. This kind of insurance is designed to protect your life savings against the risk that health issues will leave you unable to care for yourself and the need to pay for expensive assistance out of your investments. As with most insurances, when planning with LTCI, the younger you are and the healthier you are, the lower your premiums will be. One of the ways we help families plan for the worst and protect their wealth is to structure custom-designed plans for long-term care with their personal savings and investments. Every plan is different for every investor and family.

When considering options for long-term care insurance as part of your Financial Empowerment Plan, don't buy the entire farm when all you need is the barn. This happens when an insurance agent sells more bells and whistles in a policy than someone actually needs, resulting in a higher commission for the salesman but unjustified benefits and higher premiums for the policy owner.

As people live longer, the need for long-term care is growing in our society. As we age, our bodies and/or minds may begin to wear out. For an older couple, the odds are significantly higher that one or the other will need some form of long-term care at some point in his or her life. This was less a worry even a generation or two ago, but the aging population has been growing dramatically—and this will continue as baby boomers get older.

Traditional long-term care insurance, in which you pay premiums year after year in case you might need the benefit, is one option. It has become progressively more expensive, and it may be difficult or impossible to get if you wait too long or have preexisting medical conditions. As the insurance companies continually evaluate this type of coverage, policyholders often find their premiums increasing, sometimes to the point where they need to drop their insurance after years of payments because they can no longer afford the higher premiums.

One of the concerns a number of families have expressed to us is that they don't like the idea of paying LTCI premiums for a benefit that they may never need. Over the years a policyholder might pay

$20,000, $30,000, or more in total premiums, and the only return on that money would be to pay for an unfortunate and expensive stay in a facility—an outcome that nobody wants. Otherwise, the money they paid for those premiums is gone. Some buyers opt for a return-of-premium feature, but that added benefit could increase the premiums' payments significantly.

Alternatively, long-term care benefits can be provided within other types of insurance vehicles, such as annuities and life insurance, as a way to self-insure or subsidize your care. These alternative options to traditional LTCI can help families feel more secure knowing that if they never need the LTC benefit, they or their heirs will still receive the investment proceeds at their passing.

Unfortunately, it is not unusual for older people to find themselves in a situation where their income is lower but their insurance premiums increase.

When considering the types of investment tools that include a potential LTC benefit, it is vital to take the overall portfolio and finances into consideration to determine how much and where these tools make the best financial sense. And again, every family is different. In our experience, looking at the big picture, most families do not need an LTCI policy with premiums costing $5,000 a year. Rather, they would be better off with a simpler, more economical plan and/or some form of self-insuring. This type of in-depth planning is another reason to work with a full-service fiduciary advisor who will look comprehensively at the family's needs to determine the most efficient and economical plan for the family.

Unfortunately, it is not unusual for older people to find themselves in a situation where their income is lower but their insurance premiums increase. This was the case with a lady we have worked with for many years who was in her early seventies when her husband passed away. Before he passed she did everything she could to take care of him at their home, with some financial assistance from a long-term care policy he had. They had a pretty tight income of only each of their Social Securities, the lesser of which she lost when he passed. One of the monthly expenses she was struggling with paying was the long-term care policy that she had been making payments on for over fifteen years and really didn't want to lose the coverage from, especially when she received a notice from the insurance company that her premiums would be increasing. In working closely with her, her family, and the insurance company, we were able to help her negotiate a premium she could still comfortably afford, while keeping most of the policy benefits in force.

Self-Insuring

As an alternative to the traditional long-term care insurance, some families decide to self-insure and pay for some to all of the costs of LTC from their own income and investments. What could be the impact of trying to self-insure 100 percent of potential long-term care costs? Let's look at an example with an estate of $1 million: If a stay in a nursing home costs $80,000 a year, and assuming the stay lasted for five years, that would be almost half of the estate just for the cost of the nursing home, not including other costs like doctor visits, medications, and procedures. Suppose both spouses needed to enter a facility, and one had Alzheimer's and could possibly be in the facility for ten years or more. In reality, self-insuring 100 percent of the bill is not realistic for most families today; however, we've seen releveraging some investments within a portfolio help make self-insuring a feasible opportunity for a lot of investors.

If you do decide to include this concept of self-insuring as part of your long-term care planning, you should weigh all the options you have available. For some families, the best route could be to have a small long-term care policy combined with some form of asset-based coverage such as a life insurance or annuity policy that includes a long-term care benefit, and then self-insure a portion of the cost. We have worked with many families that have chosen to transfer some of the risk to an insurance company by utilizing different forms of life insurance and/or annuity vehicles. "I want the absolute best care I can find for my wife," a client once told us, "and it only makes good financial sense to leverage my money, transfer some risk to an insurance company, and end up paying pennies on the dollar, instead of dollar for dollar, for that care!"

In the unfortunate situation of needing some form of long-term care, the ultimate asset protection goal should be to avoid the possibility that the cost of care exhausts your family's assets. With so many options and alternative available, the right choice is quite often a combination of strategies that take into consideration a family's health history, longevity, and the benefits each option would provide and weighing the costs of such benefits. Long-term care insurance is often looked at as one of those insurances we really hope we never have to cash in on, as it means our health has declined considerably; however, if that time comes, families are very fortunate and blessed to have the coverage.

The Best of Intentions

The cost of long-term care, as well as the cost of insurance, can be intimidating. A lot of couples tell us if one of them have a decline in health, they will take care of each other. As comforting as that may sound, unfortunately it may not be realistic. Will the healthy spouse be able mentally and physically, not to mention financially, to take care of the ailing spouse? What happens if the caretaking spouse's health also fails?

Some families say their children will take care of them and even take them into their own homes. Again, is that realistic? The children may live miles away, with careers and family obligations of their own that could limit their time and resources. Few people can provide the amount of care that some older people will need, along with the medical expertise that may be required.

Joe and Sharon, a husband and wife we were blessed to work for many years, found out how hard this can be. Joe was a big guy, over twice the size of Sharon, and he had Alzheimer's. But Sharon vowed that she would take care of him and that he would not need to go into a nursing home. One day, however, she called us. "I need a list of good nursing homes in the area," she said.

"What's happened?"

"Well," she said, "I'm calling you from a nursing home myself. They've taken me in for rehab. I was helping Joe out of the tub, and he fell. He's in the hospital now. And I fell with him and broke my hip. The doctor says I won't be able to take care of him at home anymore."

Over the years, we have seen too many similar situations where love and devotion simply aren't enough. Being a caretaker for a loved one can be exhausting, stressful, and even physically impossible.

Trying to do as much as you can to be prepared for such unfortunate times is essential, and we strongly believe some form of long-term care asset protection is vital to have as part of every holistic and comprehensive Financial Empowerment Plan.

CHAPTER 8

STARTING WITH A SOLID FOUNDATION

You and your spouse are standing in the middle of the most beautiful piece of land you have ever seen, holding blueprints for your dream home. The construction workers begin to arrive. Imagine your surprise if the roofers showed up on site first. You would probably want to fire the general contractor for failing to organize your project in a sensible order.

That's how you should look at wealth management and income planning for retirement: it must be organized and managed in a sensible order. Just as in building your dream home, your financial house must be built on a solid foundation before the walls and roof can be built. As fiduciary advisors who specialize in retirement income planning, we serve as your project foremen or managers, making sure you're working with the right professionals, who have the right materials to build your solid financial house from the ground up.

When building a home, you want a sense of control and ownership. It wouldn't make good sense to build your dream house on somebody else's property. Likewise, your income plan should be unique to you, utilizing the right advisors, philosophy, tools, and accounts. No matter how big or small the house, the construction must always start with a solid foundation. Then it's time for the walls and windows, the rafters and shingles, the shutters and trim—in other words, the many features that make up a comprehensive financial plan. If the foundation is weak, you risk crumbling the walls and roof of your financial house.

The implementations of the Financial Empowerment Plans we build for families always start with a solid foundation that we call their "safer money," which protects the principal and provides a guaranteed monthly income for life. We then build upward with their "riskier money" to provide inflation-adjusted growth to replenish their annual income needs and continue to grow their portfolio over time. Every plan is custom-tailored to each investor and is designed to grow their overall portfolio at a level of risk and return with which they are comfortable.

Just like that of your dream home, the foundation of your financial house should be built to weather all storms. A high wind might strip off a shingle or two, but the foundation must remain solid and strong. Your portfolio must be built for any market, whether it is up, down, or sideways.

The Right Financial Builder

The financial world has three types of "builders" you can choose to work with. The first is the traditional stockbroker, who buys and sells stocks and bonds seeking generous returns for clients and possibly collecting commissions and fees. The second type of financial builder is known as a general financial advisor. Like stockbrokers, financial advisors might receive fees and commissions directly from their clients' portfolios, as well as from investment product companies, for selling their products. However, these types of advisors generally have access to a broader range of investment products, such as mutual funds, variable annuities, unit investment trusts, REITS, hedge funds, and more. As knowledgeable, experienced, and trustworthy as these types of advisors may be, they very well could have limitations or restrictions as to the tools, products, and solutions they can provide.

The third type is a fiduciary Investment Advisor Representative, or IAR, serving as a full-service designer, architect, and builder to most efficiently get you into and through your successful and awesome retirement. Most IARs are independent and aren't controlled by a broker-dealer with potentially limited and restricted options or solutions to help families. As fiduciaries, IARs are held to the highest standard in the financial industry.

Since they are independent, most IARs work from an "open resource platform," meaning there are no limitations or restrictions on the products, services, or solutions they can offer. They do not have bosses telling them what they can and cannot offer or incentivizing them to push certain products and/or companies. Independent advisors are exactly that—independent. They don't work for or represent a specific product manufacturer or sales company.

At Great Lakes Investment Advisors, we are independent, fiduciary IARs. We work directly for the families we represent, not for any broker-dealers, big-box retail brokerage firms, product manufacturers, or sales companies. We work from an open resource platform, free from any limitations or restrictions from anyone telling us what we can and cannot offer the families we serve. We are paid on a flat annual fee basis, not on a commission-per-sale/transaction basis. Our focus is to educate and empower families to make better decisions with their hard-earned money, as together we design, implement, and continually monitor their Financial Empowerment Plans to help them fulfill their retirement dreams and goals.

Safety, Growth, Liquidity

A very simple secret we learned about investing was told to us the year we started our business, by a good friend and mentor, Chuck Lucius: "The power to making money is not losing it." Investing in the stock market can be highly rewarding, with the potential for wonderful returns. However, that high reward potential also bears a higher risk: the possibility you could lose everything. You win some; you lose some. The market gives, and the market takes away. Some say that *investing* is just a sophisticated word for gambling.

As you approach retirement, it might be a good time to reassess your finances and custom build a plan to provide more safety, less risk, less volatility, and more guaranteed income.

It might seem as if anybody can make money when the stock market is going up. A rising market is generally not much of a challenge. The greater challenge is how to keep your money protected and safe when the market is falling. How do you maintain growth, or at least protect what you have? And when you need income, how do you gain the liquidity to get access to your dollars without the declining market eroding your income and lifestyle?

Even a relatively small loss can become a substantial loss if you think of the lost growth opportunity of that money. If you lose $50,000 when you are forty-five, never to invest that money again, think of what might have been: at a return of 7 percent a year, that $50,000 would have grown to more than $750,000 by the time you were eighty-five. Your real loss was three-quarters of a million dollars.

That's why safety and protecting your principal are essential considerations in managing your wealth into and through retirement. When you balance safety with solid growth and enough liquidity to meet your income needs, you can achieve a happy and successful retirement. A good rule of thumb is this: take the least amount of risk possible to generate enough income to support your retirement lifestyle, with enough growth to stay ahead of inflation.

It is very important, once again, to assess the tools that you have used to get you to this point. The tools of the accumulation years—the mutual funds, stocks, variable annuities—may very well have served their purpose getting you to retirement. As you approach retirement, it might be a good time to reassess your finances and custom build a plan to provide more safety, less risk, less volatility, and more guaranteed income. This is where we help families custom build their very own Financial Empowerment Plan to provide them with a smoother ride into and through retirement.

Arranging Your Buckets

As we help families plan their retirement income, most have expressed to us they feel most comfortable and confident knowing they will have guaranteed paychecks coming in to cover their expenses for as long as they'll live. When building income streams for later in retirement, it's very important to account for inflation. After all, a loaf of bread, a carton of eggs, and a gallon of gas are all certain to cost more as the years go by. Therefore, it is even more comforting if you can build some guaranteed pay raises into your retirement income plan.

Most pensions nowadays, if you're lucky enough to even have one, do not include a cost-of-living adjustments over time. As for the Social Security leg of your retirement stool, the government has a way of skipping or scrimping on that adjustment, as we've seen 0 percent to very little annual increases over the last decade. Without some form of hedge against inflation and built-in annual pay increases in retirement, you're taking on additional risk that your benefits will erode.

We show families how to leverage their investments to both supplement their other sources of retirement income and provide automatic annual increases in pay—raises, if you will. In that way, they can at least keep pace with inflation, and preferably even stay ahead of it. In designing income plans for families, we use a simple bucket system to map out and plan their annual and lifetime income streams.

Here's a simple example: imagine three buckets for your money, each with a different purpose. You fill the first bucket with enough to supply you with five years of income, and that is the bucket you will use for living expenses as you head into retirement. That money will be readily accessible and should be invested very conservatively, as short-term income is the main objective, rather than long-term growth.

The plan for the second bucket is not to access it for the first five years, except for emergencies, as this bucket's purpose is to replenish the first bucket when you have drained it. It will kick in to provide you with income for the next five years. If this is done properly, you should even be able to get a cost-of-living adjustment, a raise in pay, from this bucket over your previous year's pay. This bucket will still be invested fairly conservatively, as the plan will be to access it in a relatively short period of time. So you won't want to take on too much short- or long-term risk.

The third bucket can be invested at a more moderate risk level, aiming for higher returns over a longer term. The plan is to not have to access this bucket of money until after the first two five-year buckets have been depleted—so roughly ten years or so, unless, again, there are emergencies.

The more buckets you have, the more aggressive or opportunistic the longer-term ones can be invested in an effort to earn greater returns over longer periods of time. As the time approaches when you would consider accessing the funds in these longer-term buckets for income, you should dial back your risk level to more moderate and eventually conservative and income-driven.

Designing an income plan that will replenish and grow over time has sometimes been referred to as laddering and is used to provide a consistent, reliable retirement income with regular raises in income— guaranteed. Each account, or bucket, can be set up for different levels of risk, return, flexibility, and control.

Some retirees figure that instead of designing and utilizing such an income plan, they can just put their money in the market and pull out the income they need as necessary. This can work fairly well as long as the markets are going up. Unfortunately, as we all know, the markets don't always go up. During downturns, which can happen fast and often, investors may be forced to either reduce their income and lifestyle or begin spending down their nest egg at a much faster pace than they had planned—which could even cause them to run out of money at some point in life. The families we serve have found comfort over the years knowing they don't have to worry about that happening to them no matter which way the markets are moving.

Let's look at the sort of investments that might be placed in each of those buckets. The first bucket, which you are using for immediate income, is basically cash. This is liquid, accessible money—your savings and checking accounts, short-term CDs, annuities. These funds need to be available to you right away if and when you need them.

The second bucket is designed to mature in five years as a means of supplementing or replenishing your income. This bucket could be set up to provide a certain number of dollars guaranteed for the rest of your life to hedge against inflation. You will need that money to be secure because it must be there for you once the first bucket has been drained. We suggest putting only enough money in this bucket to accomplish your income goal so that you will have more assets for other uses and be leveraged for more long-term growth over time.

The plan for the third bucket is for it to grow for those ten years to replenish the income from bucket two, as well as be accessible if you should need additional income within those ten years. With that length of time, you can afford to be a little more aggressive in hopes of better returns over the longer time frame of the ten years. You could use a variety of tools, combining, for example, the safety of annuities with market investments to capture more potential for long-term growth. Beyond the first three buckets, you might have others for time frames even further out. That money could be invested more heavily in the markets because it would have more time to recover from any potential down periods where you suffered losses. This should be money you don't plan on touching until later in retirement, if it is even needed at all, or it could even end up being some of the legacy you pass on to your heirs.

Overall, this type of bucket investment system is designed to ensure a consistent, reliable income, along with the raises you might need to battle inflation, into and through a successful retirement.

Based on how much income you will need over your retirement years, the bucket system divides up and invests your money accordingly.

For families looking for a guaranteed income stream from their investments during retirement, it's vital to use the right vehicles, ones that are designed to provide guaranteed income. To us, it sure seems pretty difficult to generate a guaranteed income from a nonguaranteed account or investment. You may see mutual funds that are called income funds, or even have the word "income" in their names, when in reality they may not truly provide an investor a guaranteed income stream and may come with more risk than you're willing to take with your income. In our opinion, such investments aren't necessarily the best investments if you truly need income, especially guaranteed income.

When designing such bucket systems, each family's objectives, goals, and financial position are unique, and should be considered to determine the amount of income the family will need, the timing and duration of the income, and the level of safer and riskier investments they should own. Families that have a higher tolerance for risk can afford to have more of their money in investments designed for greater returns over the long haul, which inherently take on more risk. Families that don't have the stomach for as much risk should focus on investing in more conservative, even principal-protected, investments and tools.

Annuities and Life Insurance

Commission-based brokers, or sales agents, might favor or avoid certain products depending upon how much they get paid and what their bosses are suggesting or mandating they push and sell. As true fiduciaries we provide the best of the best advice and products for our clients based on what they are trying to accomplish. In analyzing clients' needs, we consider the wide range of tools and investments in the marketplace—anything from CDs, money markets, and savings accounts to stocks, bonds, mutual funds, ETFs, REITs, and insurance products like annuities and life insurance.

An annuity is an agreement with an insurance company in which you give the company your money with the understanding that at some point you will ask for a return of your money back with some form of interest. You could get your money back in a lump sum, or it might come in a guaranteed monthly, quarterly, or annual paycheck for as long as you or your spouse lives. For example, you pay the insurance company $100,000, and let's say five years later you decide to cash in. If the annuity is out of its surrender charge schedule, you could receive all the money you put in plus any gains—or, in the case of variable annuities, minus any potential losses you may have incurred. Or you could start getting a regular paycheck based on the annuity value, which can be structured over a certain time period and even up to as long as you live.

Annuities, like ice cream, come in many flavors. There are different annuities designed for different objectives. There are fixed annuities, fixed indexed annuities, and variable annuities, and these come in either single premium or flexible premium and either immediate or deferred income. Some annuities begin guaranteed income payments immediately, while others offer more income the longer you wait before you turn the income stream on. Some are designed for more growth potential instead of a guaranteed income stream. Some seek to deliver the maximum death benefit or inheritance to beneficiaries.

When you use the appropriate annuity to provide lifelong income, the checks will not stop as long as you live, even if you run out of money in the account. Essentially, your account balance could go to $0, but your income checks would continue as long as you're alive. With other investments, such as stocks, bonds, mutual funds, and CDs, obviously any income payments stop when you run out of money, end of story. Properly structured annuity payments, however, continue for life under the agreed contractual terms. This is a pretty cool feature of the properly structured annuity—you can run out of money, but you can never run out of income.

Not every annuity is right for everybody or for all their money. Over the years we have seen quite a few investors with variable annuities with high risk and fees that in our opinion aren't always in an investor's best interest. Variable annuities, or any investment with such higher risk, might be better suited for the accumulation stage of life rather than the preservation and income phase.

On the other hand, we have found some fixed indexed annuities to be much more appropriate for the preservation and income phases of retirement planning. Fixed indexed annuities offer the potential for a decent rate of return based on the positive returns of a stock market index such as the S&P 500, while guaranteeing and protecting the principal from any stock market losses. Most fixed indexed annuities do not have up-front or annual internal fees unless an optional income or death benefit rider is added. However, there may be early surrender fees imposed should the annuity owner chose to withdraw more in a year than allowed penalty free from the company.

Over the years we have heard a lot of good and bad comments about annuities, and yes, there are definitely some terrible annuities out there—in our experience there are also a lot of annuities that aren't bad products. It's like the old saying—"One bad apple can spoil the bunch." We have seen a lot of situations where, unfortunately, an annuity, or just the wrong flavor of annuity, was sold to the wrong investor or for the wrong reason. When this happens, it tends to make the annuity—or any investment, for that matter—seem like a bad investment.

"Don't fall in love with the investments or the tools, and don't hate them because of their name," we tell our clients. Focus on and fall in love with the benefits the annuity provides that help you accomplish your retirement goals and dreams. Just remember not to get caught up on an investment like an annuity because of its name; it's the outcome and benefits that will help you live a happy, successful retirement.

So much depends on your purposes, expectations, and situation in life. Over the years we have been the first to tell some families that certain investments such as annuities might not be in their best interests; however, we have also helped many other families incorporate annuities into the successful implementation of their Financial Empowerment Plan. When the benefit from a certain type of investment or annuity makes the best financial sense, we believe it is a wonderful planning tool for the appropriate portion of a portfolio.

Another alternative asset class that we have found to be often misunderstood and underutilized in retirement is life insurance. Most people's idea of life insurance is to pay the lowest premium for the highest death benefit, as in the traditional life insurance whereby nobody gets the payout or proceeds until someone dies. In this sense, it's more like death insurance, because someone must die before a benefit is paid out.

Just like municipal bonds and Roth IRAs, life insurance has helped a lot of families reap tax-free benefits and income in retirement. Such tax-free benefits can come from properly structured life insurance, known as LIRP (life insurance retirement plans). By structuring and incorporating LIRPs properly into your overall retirement planning, you can add tremendous value by providing retirement income, a death benefit, and provisions for long-term care expenses—all potentially 100 percent income tax-free.

Weathering All Storms

The families we serve often ask how much they can withdraw from their portfolio in retirement and not have to worry about running out of money. This is a very common concern today, especially after the stock market corrections of 2001–2003 and 2008–2009, paired with declining bond yields and the loss of a lot of stocks paying dividends.

Historically, the level of withdrawal considered to be safe was a lot higher. An article published by *FIDELITY* in 2018 suggested you should be okay withdrawing 4 to 5 percent of your portfolio for income in retirement.[1] When we help families determine what's appropriate, it's not a one-size-fits-all number. Families differ in their lifestyles, investments, goals and objectives, risk tolerances, income needs, and much more.

Which would you prefer—a 95 percent chance that you will not run out of money in retirement, or a 100 percent chance? Would you get on a plane if the airline told you that you had a 95 percent chance of landing safely? At this phase of life, you cannot afford to make costly mistakes with your life savings. You have one shot at retirement, so you have to build a strong Financial Empowerment Plan and get it right the first time—after all, most only get one shot at retirement.

We often ask families, "Do you want your retirement income and lifestyle to be dictated by the whipsaw ups and downs of the stock market, or would you be more comfortable with knowing you have a consistent, reliable income stream every month no matter what type

---

1   "How Can I Make My Retirement Savings Last?," Fidelity Viewpoints, July 21, 2020, https://www.fidelity.com/viewpoints/retirement/how-long-will-savings-last.

of wild animal the unpredictable stock market decides to be?" The three-, five-, and ten-year average returns of a mutual fund might look good, but what about the years in between that you don't see? When we looked at most retail mutual fund prospectuses that included the years 2008 and 2009 in their historical average returns, all of their three-, five-, and ten-year average returns were positive—yet the overall stock market, and particularly the funds they owned, were down quite significantly in 2008. If you were to retire just before a downturn like that, you could face an immediate loss of a major portion of your portfolio. If you lose a third of your portfolio, are you willing to give up a third of your income and your lifestyle?

Don't just hope that things will turn out all right. Know that they will. You should be able to expect the comfort of a guaranteed retirement income. We show our most successful families how they can live comfortably in retirement without worrying whether their gamble in the stock market is enough or too much.

Your retirement dreams should not be vulnerable to the unpredictable and often unfortunate swings of the stock market. The income from the third leg of your financial lifestyle stool—your own savings and investments—should be built primarily on guarantees. Your income supports your lifestyle. A guaranteed income means a guaranteed lifestyle. You deserve peace of mind, knowing that your financial foundation is solid. Your Financial Empowerment Plan, with the appropriate balance of safety, income, and risk, should be built to weather all storms.

CHAPTER 9

PASSING IT ON

AT THE TIME WE FIRST began to think about writing a book, the singer Prince had just died from an accidental overdose of opioid painkillers. This was a man who was deeply concerned about controlling his image and publicity. He was a very private individual, but he passed away without a will or a trust or any wealth-transfer documents, subjecting all of his assets and his entire estate to the probate court process, for all of the world to see.

Estimates put the value of the Prince estate at about $300 million, not including the potential worth of a collection of unpublished music, with about half the total due in taxes and the remainder under the control of heirs.

Estate planning and having the appropriate estate-planning documents in place are not only concerns of the "rich and famous" but ultimately a responsibility we should all take on.

Thinking about estate planning is something most people have a tendency to procrastinate about, especially when they are younger and in good health. It is something they figure they can do tomorrow, or "when we need it." If Prince had put his assets in a trust, his heirs would have owned everything in that trust on the day he passed away, without the expense, publicity, long delays, hassles, and headaches quite often associated with probate court. The money could have passed from generation to generation, or to charity, or be managed as the singer thought best. But unfortunately, Prince hadn't done any estate planning.

Estate planning and having the appropriate estate-planning documents in place are not only concerns of the "rich and famous" but ultimately a responsibility we should all take on, and we should have the appropriate planning done while we are healthy and able. Many families will need more thorough, in-depth, and comprehensive planning and documents; however, simpler forms of wills and power of attorney documents may very well be all a person or family needs to accomplish their goals. The completer the planning we have done and in place before we either need care in a home or ultimately pass away, the quicker, smoother, and simpler it will be for our loved ones to take care of us when we are sick and ultimately pass on.

Estate planning can entail different processes and formalities depending on each family's situation: some people and families may be fine with a simple will, simple power of attorney documents, and some account titling and beneficiary updating. In our experience we've met and worked with attorneys who felt it was in a family's best interest to just have simple wills and power of attorney documents in place, such that when they die the attorney settles the estate with the heirs through the process of probate court. We have also met a lot of families, and attorneys, over our last nineteen years as investment advisors who consider a more comprehensive revocable living trust to be in their best interests, after some discussions about the family's goals and objectives, or per an attorney's suggestions. The more organized and comprehensive plans we can design and build while we are healthy and alive, the easier and more efficient any unfortunate health situation, and ultimately our death, will be for our loved ones to cope with.

Wanting to avoid federal estate taxes has historically been a reason for utilizing some form of trust in estate planning. The federal estate tax is a tax that can certainly effect families of higher net worth, but the federal exemption has been set at such a high level—for 2020, it is $11.58 million for an individual and twice that for a couple—that many families do not have to worry about this potential tax burden. In years when the federal estate tax exemption limit wasn't as high, or even now for higher net worth families that might be nearing or above this amount, proper estate planning with a revocable living trust could help shelter their assets from this tax.

Other potential tax bills that quite often get overlooked are those building up inside tax-deferred accounts such as IRAs, 401(k)s, 403(b)s, and others. We have met and worked with a lot of families over the years that have done a really good job of saving for their retirement and investing in these types of tax-deferred retirement accounts. The benefit of not having to pay taxes on the amount contributed to these accounts, as well as any and all growth over the years, can be a very beneficial and powerful component of building wealth in our accumulation phase of life. The day will come, however, when that money must be taxed. As we saw in Chapter 6, it can be a particularly damaging tax bomb if the money is left for the next generation. In our experience, even against better advice, we have seen many heirs take the money as a lump sum, immediately losing 20 or 30 percent or more to taxes, even when they might have continued to stretch the tax deferral over longer time frames, potentially receiving a lot more money. How these types of accounts will be passed along, the choices our beneficiaries might have, and the amount of taxes that will be owed and when are all important aspects to consider in a comprehensive estate plan.

The Leverage of Life Insurance

Advanced tax and estate planning often makes use of different forms of life insurance to ease the potential tax burden growing within tax-deferred accounts. Let's say you have a $500,000 IRA. If your children inherited that as a lump sum, they would pay a tax of perhaps 35 percent or more on that amount of income. In anticipation of that big tax bill, we have shown many of our most successful families how they can take out a life insurance policy with enough death benefit value to cover that tax expense for their heirs. In effect, you are releveraging a small portion of your money to purchase a tax-protection plan for your heirs. For pennies on the dollar, you pay off Uncle Sam and ensure your IRAs go to your heirs in the most tax-efficient way. Utilizing life insurance for more tax-efficient wealth transfer is a very common but often overlooked advanced planning strategy that can be extremely valuable to a family and the heirs.

Wills and Trusts

A will is a very simple and basic estate-planning document for passing on assets that an individual or couple can put into play. Having a will, however, may not always avoid probate. Most estates with simple wills may end up still going through some form of probate court process.

Think of a will as a dormant, or dead, if you will, document that comes alive when the person passes away, and as a direction or wish list of what they want to happen with their stuff—whom they would like their stuff to go to.

A revocable living trust, by contrast, is more of a "living" estate-planning document that allows the grantor to potentially have more control and power over who will receive their assets and when. Having a revocable living trust in some respects allows you to make the decisions while you are alive and able that otherwise attorneys and judges may end up making for you through probate court if you just have a will. Ultimately you have more power and control over who will receive your assets and when with revocable living trusts. If they are properly written, funded, and administered over your lifetime, utilizing revocable living trusts can be a good way to avoid the full-blown probate court process.

A potential big advantage of a revocable living trust could be the overall expense savings. The cost of probate can amount to 2 to 5 percent of the overall value of the estate. That money goes to the lawyers and the courts before the heirs see a dime. Most people would prefer that their children be the beneficiary of their life's work before attorneys, judges, and the court system. Probate court could also be very time-consuming. Anyone who has had experience with the courts knows that most things in courts don't happen fast and are often set up on thirty-, sixty-, or ninety-day time frames. Probate court cases can potentially stretch out a long time, particularly in situations where someone is contesting the will or any aspect of the distribution of an estate. Facing a postponement in the courts can feel a lot like sitting in a taxicab at a red light or traffic jam and watching the meter just keep ticking and accumulating the longer you have to wait. Such delays could add up to more expenses going into the probate court and away from the beneficiaries of the estates.

Probate court is also public record. Anybody can go to the courthouse and request documentation or even sit in the courtroom and listen while your private affairs are aired. The public will know who is involved, who owns what, and who gets how much. Most people want more privacy for their family than that. Anyone attending the hearing can raise a hand to contest the case. Creditors of one sort or another can come out of the woodwork, as in "I painted their garage ten years ago, and they owe me five hundred dollars for it." Some such claims could be valid; however, we have heard many unfortunate stories from families who've had false claims raised in the probate court process, which could ultimately take up more time and cost more money before the estate can be settled.

Most families do not want to put the children through such expenses and aggravation. That is why some form of a trust often is a good idea. When set up properly, a trust can potentially protect against claims from creditors and against claims made in lawsuits and divorces. Setting one up can be relatively inexpensive. We've seen trust costs run between $1,500 and $4,000, which could be money well spent and potentially could save you far more down the road. Most full trusts are all-encompassing umbrella packages that include the will and trust, powers of attorney for healthcare and finances, and a healthcare directive, often called a living will, personal property distribution, and a pour-over will designed to catch any assets that might have slipped through the funding process.

After setting up a trust, it is vital to assure it is properly administered and, most importantly, funded. For example, you might put your home in the trust with some form of deeded ownership. If your home is only in your will, it will most likely have to go to probate court. With a trust, it may be able to go directly to your heirs. Another benefit of using a trust might be to limit what one child gets from the estate and make special arrangements for another, otherwise known as controlled distribution or inheritance. For example, perhaps you have a child who has a disability and is incapable of handling money—and who might lose state or federal benefits if they were to receive an inheritance. The trust can specify and place conditions on how the assets will be distributed and over what period of time so as to allow your child to benefit from their inheritance without the risk of being kicked off of their state- or federally funded aid. You might even provide a match to whatever your children earn each year, as an incentive for hard work. You can reward milestones in their lives, distributing funds upon marriage, for example, or college graduation. You can specify that they must stretch an inheritance by taking an income gradually over their lifetimes. These are just a few examples where we have seen families utilize benefits of controlled distribution with a trust that most likely couldn't be accomplished with a simple will.

A revocable living trust, with everything under one umbrella, can be changed at any time by the grantors of the trust, as the word *revocable* indicates. You can change the beneficiaries, you can sell the home and buy another, and you can easily make many other adjustments inside a revocable trust while you are alive and able. Wills and/ or trusts can be essential parts of your overall estate planning—which one is best for your family will ultimately depend on your situation and goals. That's where the professional guidance of appropriately licensed attorneys is a must, as we are not licensed to give legal and tax advice—we know just enough about that stuff to be dangerous and know it's in all of our best interests to seek out the guidance of an estate-planning attorney.

Charitable Giving

We have helped some of our charitable families set up such solutions as donor-advised funds and charitable trusts, funded with different investments like stocks, mutual funds, ETFs, real estate, annuities, and/or life insurance. Charitable giving doesn't have to wait until you are dead. We help a lot of our families enjoy the benefits and personal satisfactions that come with charitable giving by releveraging some of their investments, or even a portion of their returns, into charitable solutions that they can divvy out to the charity or charities of their choice when they desire, as well as get an immediate tax deduction for the amount put into the solution.

Let's take a look at how a family used just one of those various strategies—the charitable remainder trust—to accomplish their goals. This couple owned a farm that had increased tenfold in value by virtue of its location. The property was next to a business that wanted to expand and had no other space to grow. The family was able to sell their land to the business next door for $750,000.

The high dollar amount of the sale also came with a potential high dollar tax problem. The land had increased in value quite a bit over time from what the family purchased it for years ago, which meant they had a potentially large capital gains tax bill owed to the IRS.

We introduced them to an estate-planning attorney, who evaluated their potentially big tax problem and came up with a solution: they should give away the $750,000 that they had received for the property. It would be a nice piece of change that some charity would be pleased to accept.

Give it all away? You can imagine the look of doubt on the faces of people who hear such a suggestion. Why would they give away so much money when they may need it themselves to live on in retirement and also might want to leave their children a nice inheritance?

But the benefits of this gifting solution really made good financial sense for this family. The attorneys suggested that they set up a charitable remainder trust, donating the money to whatever causes or institutions had been most meaningful to the family. The money would not go immediately to charity. Instead, for the rest of their lives, the couple could continue to manage the money within the trust and make use of the income that it produced. The money would not go to the charity until they both passed away. However, the couple would immediately receive a major tax deduction for the $750,000 that they were donating.

But what about their children? Wouldn't that mean that the children lose out on a $750,000 inheritance? Providing a tax-free inheritance to their kids also made good financial sense. They used part of their annual income from the trust to pay the premiums on a $750,000 life insurance policy, listing their children as the beneficiaries. The life insurance was a second-to-die policy, meaning that it would pay out benefits to the heirs only when both husband and wife had passed.

That strategy resulted in the charity receiving $750,000, which the charity received tax free by virtue of its charitable exemption. Upon their mom and dad's deaths, the children will also receive $750,000 from the insurance proceeds, which will also pass to them income tax-free. This advanced planning strategy allowed the couple to releverage three-quarters of a million dollars of their assets to provide them with income they needed over their retirement and provide a very healthy tax-free legacy for their heirs when they pass away, while at the same time benefiting the charity and a lot of other families' lives—it meant so much to them to be able to do so much more good in the world.

We offer that example to illustrate how a wise strategy for handling your estate can serve your family well for generations. Quite often we discuss such advanced planning strategies with the families we work with and refer them to the appropriate professionals to help fulfill their plan. Sometimes new families are surprised when we talk about estate and tax matters, telling us that their current/previous broker never talked about such things—which may be because their broker did not embrace the fiduciary, comprehensive approach to financial planning but rather sold them mutual funds and other products for commission.

The reality is you do actually have an estate plan, even if you have never drafted one, and even if you have never thought about it. If you have not taken steps to create your own plan, don't worry—the government has one for you. Chances are, a plan prepared and fulfilled by the government may not be in you and your family's best interests. So that you are not subject to the mercy of the government's plan, when you work with a fiduciary advisor who by law must look out for your best interests, your estate, legacy, and tax planning should all be integral parts of your overall Financial Empowerment Plan.

WHILE THERE'S TIME

You may have hit a few home runs in your time, maybe even an investment grand slam, and those do make for good talk around the bonfire. But as you head into retirement and think about your score, it was probably the base hits, the singles and the doubles, that brought you around the diamond most successfully in the game of getting to retirement.

Heading into retirement is like stepping to the plate once again. Will you be swinging for the fences and listening for the cheers from the crowd as you cross the plate with another long-ball home run? Or will your retirement be a little smoother, getting through base by base, alert to every motion on the field?

Most of the families we work with find retirement so much more enjoyable just swinging for singles and doubles. Sometimes they do connect for a big home run, but their primary game plan is to play it a little safer. When you are not trying to hit every ball with your hardest swing and knock it out of the park, you will be far less likely to strike out. Early in your working game, neither a strikeout nor a homer really affected you too much, because you were in the early innings and had a lot of time on your side in the game. But as you are nearing or just into retirement, every pitch really counts. At this phase of the game, the last thing you want is a financial strikeout.

Baseball is a beautiful metaphor for life's journey. At every step are dangers and risks, with safe havens all around where we can retreat until the next big opportunity. If you get tagged out at first base in the early innings, it is a disappointment, and chances are you'll get to bat again. But if that happens as you're rounding third base and heading for home plate in the top or bottom of the ninth, your game might just be over.

In every chapter of this book, we have emphasized the need to use the philosophies, tools, and advisors for this next phase of your life—a happy, successful, awesome retirement. Just as a ball team's manager might pull his starter late in a game to go with a pitcher who's built and paid to be more of a closer, at this stage in your game, it might be time to switch it up and transition out of the strategies and investments that you used in the accumulation phase of your life. It just might be in your best interest to change it up a little bit, to bring in some new players who by law must look out for your best interest and might use some different tools and strategies to help you most successfully close out with your own winning retirement.

Just like you, baseball coaches struggle with pulling their ace starters or even trading some of their most tenured players and bringing in new ones. Making that switch can be hard to do. You may even feel disloyal. But remember that your goal is to win the game for yourself and for your family and to make sure you are doing what's in your best interest to live your happy and successful, awesome retirement, not anybody else's.

"What am I going to say to my broker?" Bruce, a prospective client who was nearing retirement asked us when we suggested he needed a different approach. "See, he's a good friend too. I go to church with him. We golf together. I hear what you're saying. I know I need to be handling these things differently, but what am I going to tell him?"

Working with families and helping them organize and manage their affairs for this next phase of their lives—into and through a happy, successful, awesome retirement—we know it's not always a fun and easy transition to make. We get questions like that last one quite often, and our answer is simple: our objective with every family we meet is to educate and empower them to make better decisions with their hard-earned money. The education is often that there are different tools and strategies that may be more powerful and efficient for a happier, more successful retirement than the ones they are currently using. The empowerment is often that they feel so confident and comfortable that any changes we suggest are truly in their best interest, that there's nothing wrong with what they are currently doing, and that there's nobody to be mad at or blame and definitely no hard feelings to be had or enemies to be made for them simply doing what truly is in their best interest.

"Bruce, by now you know we help families build their very own personalized Financial Empowerment Plans that are designed to weather all storms, which sometimes means adding new and replacing old. But only if it makes perfectly good financial sense and is one hundred percent in your best interest. We're not here to tell you to hate or fire your current broker. We're simply here to help you take everything your current broker has done so well for you and Yvonne and elevate it to the next level so you can truly live the happy, successful, awesome retirement you told us you've always dreamed of."

"Thank you so much, Carl and Jason. This is exactly what Yvonne and I have always been looking for. You're absolutely right. He's a great guy; he's done us well, and I am sure he'll understand and respect that we just have to make some changes that are in our best interest for retirement, and you're just the guys we want to work with."

That was four years ago. Bruce was right. His broker fully understood why Bruce and Yvonne were making the move. He tells us now that he and Yvonne have found such peace of mind in knowing with confidence that they will have enough money throughout their retirement years to travel, volunteer, spend time with their grandkids, and live the happy and successful retirement they always dreamed of. After our last review, Bruce said, "Carl, we just want you and Jason to know, we couldn't have done all this without you."

Tim and Sally were a family we had been working for since the year we launched our business together as father and son. At that time Sally was ready to retire, so we helped her to organize and consolidate her finances. Tim told us that he expected to work for about five more years. They were relatively young and active and doing well financially. We started the implementation of their Financial Empowerment Plan with an initial five-year plan, with Sally being in retirement and Tim retiring in the fifth year.

About three and a half years later, at one of our annual reviews, they were all smiles. "I can't believe we've gotten to this point already!" Sally said. "You set out on a five-year plan, and here we are, three and a half years into it, and you have helped us accomplish our goals a year and a half early."

"That's right," Tim added. "Just look at these figures. I'm all set to retire now." They were right. They had met their objectives, and nothing was stopping them from taking that next step. Over the next year, they realized a longtime dream—to build their retirement home in Florida.

Not long after the house was completed, I received a devastating call that Tim's doctor had discovered Tim had cancer. He was fading fast. We were still their financial advisors, so we were in touch with them regularly by telephone. It got to the point where Tim no longer could get up to use the phone. We did some video conferences, which he was able to join while staying in bed.

> **We are in the business of helping people to build their dreams while they still have time.**

And then one day Sally called to tell us that Tim had passed. She wanted us to know that Tim, in his last hours, with his family at his bedside, had told them that their dreams could not have come true had it not been for us. He had asked Sally to continue working with us because he knew in his heart that she would be in the best of care with us looking out for her best interest—and we have done just that.

In the six months before we began writing this book, five of our clients passed away—three of whom had been with us since the founding of our business. Those calls were among the toughest moments of our careers. It is hard to say goodbye, but hearing such expressions of appreciation is deeply gratifying, and it helps us and the families get through the worst times.

We become quite fond of the families we serve. We grieve with them, and we rejoice with them. We are in the business of helping people to build their dreams while they still have time. That is why we do what we do.

ABOUT THE AUTHORS

JASON F. CRYDERMAN

As THE PRESIDENT and cofounder of Great Lakes Investment Advisors, Jason Cryderman is focused on helping clients work toward their retirement dreams through a well-thought-out strategy for retirement income.

Jason began his career in the insurance and financial services industry in 1998. His passion is working with retirees and those preparing for retirement to develop and monitor investment and income strategies tailored to meet their life goals. He has helped hundreds of families appropriately manage their investment exposure to taxes, fees, and risk.

Jason is a licensed fiduciary Investment Adviser Representative (IAR). He has passed the Series 65 securities exam and holds licenses in life and health insurance as well as variable annuities. He has a bachelor's degree from Michigan State University. Jason stays active in volunteering throughout his community; he is a member in superior standing with the National Ethics Association, is a member of the

Midland Area Chamber of Commerce and the Better Business Bureau, and is on the board of the MSU Alumni Club of Midland County and his Township Board of Appeals.

Jason and his wife, Amy, live in Sanford, Michigan, with their two daughters, Alexis and Joslyn; their son, Carson; and their loving yellow lab, Gunner. They enjoy spending time together as a family, including all kinds of sports, outdoor activities, snowmobiling, and boating. Jason also enjoys hockey, golf, fishing, and hunting.

CARL A. CRYDERMAN

As the vice president of Great Lakes Investment Advisors, Carl is a financial planner specializing in retirement planning and asset preservation for retirees and those preparing for retirement.

Jason and Carl have been helping retirees and those preparing to retire reach their financial, retirement, and estate planning goals for almost two decades. Carl has built a reputation among the families he serves and fellow colleagues as a personally engaged problem solver who provides exceptional customer service. Carl is legally bound to uphold the highest level of fiduciary standards when providing investment advice to his clients. When working with clients, attorneys, CPAs, other advisors, and caregivers, Carl's approach is all-inclusive, transparent, and education-based.

Carl has been a mentor, coach, and advisor for asset accumulation, asset protection, and retirement income for over twenty years. He is a member in superior standing with the National Ethics Association, in addition to being a member of the Better Business Bureau, Midland Chamber of Commerce, and American Veterans.

Carl and his wife, Carole, along with their two dogs, Pablo and Bo, are longtime residents of Midland, Michigan. When not serving his valued clients or enjoying time with their family, Carl and Carole enjoy traveling, camping, kayaking, biking, hunting, and fishing.

Jason, Carl, and their team at Great Lakes Investment Advisors are widely recognized in Michigan and beyond as specialists in retirement planning.

Printed in the USA
CPSIA information can be obtained
at www.ICGtesting.com
JSHW012039140824
68134JS00033B/3151